21 Days

To

Creating Your Dream Life

A guide to opening doors and thoughts you never thought possible before...

Stephen J. Mark

Dream Board Publications LLC

Atlanta, Georgia

2

Published by

Dream Board Publications LLC, 1353 Riverstone Parkway, Suite 120-252, Canton, GA 30114

Copyright © Stephen J. Mark, 2008

All rights reserved. The above information forms this copyright notice: All rights reserved under the Pan-American and International Copyright Conventions.

This book may not be reproduced in whole or in part, in any form or by any means, electronic or mechanical, including photocopying, recording, or by any information storage and retrieval system now known or hereafter invented, without written permission from the Publisher.

Printed in the United States of America

Library of Congress Control Number: 2008903241

ISBN-13: 978-0-9816275-0-2

ISBN-10:   0-9816275-0-1

Visit us on the web to order more books or for distribution contacts!

www.stephenmark.com

www.dreamboardpublications.com

BOOKS ARE AVAILABLE AT QUANTITY DISCOUNTS WHEN USED TO PROMOTE PRODUCTS OR SERVICES . FOR INFORMATION PLEASE WRITE TO MARKETING DEPARTMENT, DREAM BOARD PUBLICATIONS LLC, 1353 RIVERSTONE PARKWAY, SUITE 120-252, CANTON, GEORGIA 30114

Contents

Acknowledgements

There are a number of people I would to thank for their input into this book. First, I would like to thank my wife for her belief and support during this project from its point of conception to final delivery. Next, I would like to thank my mom and dad, friends, and neighbors for their love and support while working on this project.

Thank you and I Love You!

I'd like to thank Tony Robbins and Joseph McClendon III for all their inspiration. Tony, thank you for referencing usable life tools at your seminars. You have always been an inspiration. Both of your inspiring stories have made me change the way I think, feel, and go about life everyday!

A Special Thank You to the Both of you!

I would also like to thank all of the people who have shared their stories in this book, though all names have been changed to protect identities. Any resemblances are coincidental. Without your stories and your own desire for a change in your life, this book would be full of empty, boring pages.

On the technical side, I want to thank Ann Clayton for her graphic design expertise in designing the cover. And to my best friend, Mike Clayton, I want to thank him for his support and consistent brotherhood throughout the years. Lisa Oliver, for all her help and expertise in bringing the material and information together in a recognizable format. I couldn't have done it without you!

Last, but definitely not least, I want to thank you, my readers, because *it is your desire to live the life you want to live* that makes my life all the more worthwhile.

Thank You!

                    www.stephenmark.com

Foreword

It is sometimes easy to forget in the world of self-help and self-improvement that every person who looks for something different in their lives all want different things. So their desires are similar, but their measure of success and of achievement are all different. A wealthy banker might want more time with his or her family; a woman who has spent twenty years raising her children might want to go back to school or work; the student might want to travel before beginning a career; and the retiree might want to give something back to his or her community.

This book provides a model for change. It is a system that is flexible enough for you to adapt to, no matter what you want to accomplish in your life. It is also flexible enough to be useful regardless of your current circumstances. Many current self-help books will only help you achieve success in one area of your life, and they tend to include the holistic approach. I hope you will find this book far more suited to your needs than others you might have tried.

I wish you well on your journey to Creating Your Dream Life.

Preface

Are you one of those people who believe that good fortune, success, blooming health and all the perks of a wealthy lifestyle comes to a select few, who somehow have managed to win life's lottery? Are you one of life's ordinary people – humdrum job, humdrum life? Do you believe the gap between where you are and where you want to be is just too big and can never be reached?

Answer yes to any of the above and you need to read this book.

You see, too many of us think that success will always be just out of our grasp; that we will never have the good fortune to have a life that fits on the cover of Time magazine, or any publication that we enjoy. What we fail to realize is that **this type of thinking is one of the barriers that is holding us back from our success**. That's right – if you think that you can't succeed and live the life you want to live, you will be right – every time.

You see, the Universe is a wondrous place and whether you believe in it in a spiritual sense or not, the Universe has this way of looking out for you and giving you what you want, all the time. Unfortunately, too many of us spend our time complaining about what we haven't got, and don't take the time to consider that it is our complaints that are coming true in our lives - not our dreams, our desires or our goals. But I am getting ahead of myself. Suffice to say at this point – you have a lot more power to change your life, than you can ever imagine.

Have you ever heard about NLP? NLP stands for Neurolinguistic Programming, which is a personal development system devised in the 1970s. The main idea behind NLP is that it is an individual's thoughts, feelings, actions and experiences that create individual perceptions. It is this perception that impacts the way we act in our daily lives, and it is this perception that can be changed, enabling us to change our lives. WOW, if that were true, and it is, the possibilities for what you could have in your life, are endless.

You have a desire to change your life – otherwise you would not be reading this book. But I am willing to bet that you don't know how to go about it. I am also willing to bet that there is a part of you that is just a bit scared of succeeding – I mean, what would that do to your self-esteem; to your relationships with family, friends and co-workers and to the way you live your life? Change is always a scary prospect, but if you are in control of the change process, then it doesn't have to be a negative experience. This book will show you how you can control your life to the point where you are living where you want to be, and doing what you want to do, rather than what you are doing right now.

I have just one more piece of advice to give you before we begin on your journey to the life you want: Be ready for it. If you are ready, your life could change today – as you are reading this book. And it will change today, because whether you believe in the process this book will teach you, or not, your life will be forever changed because you did read this book. You have nothing to lose and everything to gain from not only reading this book, but also using it as a tool while creating a new blueprint to the life you have only dreamed of. **Let's begin.**

Introduction

Most of us spend our lives looking for "something else" regardless of where we are in our lives at any given time. We could all do with more money, more success, more time, a good relationship, any relationship, a diet that works or an easy way to stop smoking. And no matter where we look, the people we are looking at always seem to have a better life than we do.

This can cause us to feel frustration, envy, bitterness, or resignation. The feelings of frustration are based on the perception that we are not as successful as "they" are; we feel envy at the apparent easy life everyone else seems to have; we feel bitter because we believe that these other people must be so "lucky" and this feeling is often accompanied by the complaint, "how come we don't get the same breaks". Perhaps the saddest emotion this type of observation causes is that of resignation; that feeling of never being good enough, and never being capable of achieving the same happy life that everyone else has or at least that's how it is perceived within ourselves while watching other people around us.

Nothing impacts us more in life than our perceptions of life and people around us, and how we feel about ourselves. We will talk more about perceptions in the first chapter of this book, but for now, you need to appreciate how perceptions filter everything around us. Kind of like a pair of polarized sunglasses, they only allow certain wavelengths of light to come through. They filter out the rest. For example, how would you feel if you had just found out that your neighbor won $100,000 in a lottery draw? Consider the table and responses on the next page:

Feeling	Response
Bitterness	"Just typical isn't it; like they need the money. They're just lucky. I suppose they will just brag around and lord over us even more now, there will be no shutting them up about this one"
Envy	"Wow, I wish I could win that amount of money. Man, I could buy all sorts of things with it – a new boat, a new car, heavens - a new life if I wanted"
Frustration	"Gosh, I am so angry, why can't I get a break like that? I have bills to pay and car repairs I can't pay for. It's not as though they needed the money anyway, why couldn't it have been me?"
Resignation	"Well of course it would happen to them– they are Mister and Misses Successful aren't they? I could never win a lottery; I can't even afford to buy a ticket. I don't know why I am surprised because they obviously deserve it more than me anyway."

Can you relate to any of the statements made by our disgruntled neighbors? Or do you have a more positive outlook on life?

Let's consider some positive responses to the same situation. See which table better describes you.

Feeling	Response
Happiness	"Wow, that is so great – they really deserve this win. I must go over and congratulate them, maybe now they will be able to afford a holiday or something special for themselves"
Surprise	"Wow, I never knew anyone that won a large sum of money like that in a lottery before. Maybe I should start buying tickets"
Genuine goodwill	"That is just wonderful. If anybody deserved to win a nice sum of money it is our neighbors. They are such nice people and I hope they can do something positive for themselves with it"
Thankfulness	"I am so pleased that the win went to such a nice family. They have had so many trials and tribulations lately, this will seem like a gift from the heavens. I am so thankful it went to a family that really needed it"

As you can see, these tables show eight completely different responses to the same situation and this is not an exhaustive list. The tables don't mention anger, hatred, anxiety, greed, or a multitude of other feelings that could be generated by the one event.

A second aspect that we can learn from this example is that our feelings regulate our responses and behavior. If I asked you to name a feeling that applied to any one of the eight responses illustrated, I am sure you would not have too much trouble working out which one was which. What if we added a behavior column to the same example? We would get something that looked like this:

Feeling	Behavior
Bitterness	Goes off to get another beer from the fridge and when he sees his neighbor later in the day he just ignores him.
Envy	Goes around to visit the neighbors to find out what they will be buying and how they will spend it, and see if there is any chance he can get some money directed his way.
Frustration	Slams around the house for a while, and then goes off to meet with some friends. Turns back up at home a lot later and smelling like booze.
Resignation	Sits quietly in his room, wondering if his life will ever get any better. But he doesn't think it will, so he is probably right.
Happiness	Whips up a batch of cookies and goes over to visit the neighbors, happy to share their good fortune and to offer congratulations.
Surprise	Starts looking at the statistics about the chance of winning the lottery and decides it probably wouldn't hurt to get a ticket even though the odds of winning are quite low, because "you have to be in it to win it".
Thankfulness	Pops round to visit the neighbors, just to say how pleased he is for them. Later he prays and gives thanks for the neighbors' good fortune.

As you can see, very different feelings give rise to very different behaviors, and each one of these feelings and subsequent actions are all a result of the perceptions that a person can have about life in general. Cognitive Behavioral Theory examines this idea in some detail – where an individuals' perceptions based on previous life experience, tarnishes or enhances all situations in present day life. Cognitive Behavioral Therapy (CBT) is founded on the idea that a person can create a far more positive life for himself if he chooses to look at the events and situations around him from a more healthy perspective.

If we accept the link between perceptions, feelings and behaviors, does this mean that there is a right way to see different situations? If we use the examples in the tables, is one of these responses the right way to view a situation? Surprisingly the answer is "no". There is no one right way to view any event or situation. There are socially acceptable ways of viewing things; there are ethical ways of viewing things; there are all sorts of ways of viewing any one situation or event, but none of them are better than any other except how that response pertains to the individual.

The one person we can't avoid in life is ourselves – we have to live with ourselves every day, even if we hide ourselves away from everybody else. To maintain our health, we need to be happy with ourselves, and it is this happiness that should be the major influence in how we respond to different situations. But so many of us have our perceptions damaged in some way to the point where we behave in a way that does not facilitate good health or peace of mind. Our negative behaviors caused by erroneous perceptions further sabotage our life to the point where we experience negative outcomes, which in turn reinforces our negative perceptions – as you can see, this causes a very negative spiral that if not stopped and reversed in any way, can lead to us being really unhappy in our lives, no matter what we do, or who we think we are.

Before we move on to the first part of this book, I want you to stop for five minutes and do something for yourself. I want you to find a quiet place where you will not be disturbed for at least five minutes. When

                    www.stephenmark.com

you are sitting quietly, I want you to close your eyes and go to that place in your mind where you can have anything and everything you want in life. This is a place where there are no limitations on how you spend your time, your money or any situation where you maybe judged by other people. We all have such a place in our mind, but we often ignore it because we feel it is too far removed from our version of reality. But in this moment, I want you to visit this place and get reacquainted with who you really are. Imagine having the perfect life with money, love, health, relationships, a career or what ever it is that you want in your ideal life.

When you are comfortable in this place in your mind, I want you to start acknowledging how this mental visit is making you feel. Do you feel calm, at peace, unhurried, or even relaxed (something that is getting harder to achieve in our hectic lifestyles)? Do you feel happy and in control of your life? You should; after all, this is your ideal life fantasy, and you have the power to create, change, edit or manipulate your fantasy world in any way that you choose.

Now I want you to shift your focus just a little bit. I want you to concentrate on the positive changes that have occurred in your body in this brief period of time, simply by spending time in your fantasy world. You will feel more alive, more open to opportunities, more rested, calm and at peace with everything around you. This is the feeling of your body being at its most balanced state, and it is through this balance and positive energy that you can change your life to the point where you can experience these feelings everyday, not just when you are asked to. Now wouldn't that be wonderful!

Part One

If Success Is So Easy,
Then Why Haven't I Got It?

Chapter One

Success Is For Other People

It's official – someone up there doesn't like me! How often have you said something like this? Every time you hear that someone you know has won money, the lotto, or any raffle; every time someone else succeeds in an area where you believe you are just mediocre; every time someone meets their soul mate while you are still alone and single on a Saturday night? It just seems like life isn't fair and everyone else gets the breaks, and not you. Did you ever stop to think that maybe it was because of the way you are thinking that things don't appear to happen to you; or that maybe they do happen to you and you just don't notice?

It is human nature to think that the grass is always greener on the other side of the fence. Unfortunately, the premise this thought is based on is actually misleading. For example, say you are admiring your neighbor's new boat over the fence. It looks expensive, shiny and new and is something you have wanted to get for as long as you can remember. If you are having a good day, your thoughts as you look at it are likely to run along the lines of "the lucky bastard, how on earth did he afford that?" If you are having a bad day, your thoughts are not likely to be as charitable or as nice.

The funny thing is, in this type of situation, your thought patterns are making a lot of assumptions. For example, you think the boat belongs to your neighbor, when in fact it might be just parked there by a friend or family member. You are assuming that even if the boat does belong to the neighbor that a) he bought it; b) he paid cash for it and c) that it was expensive. From your side of the fence, there is no factual evidence to support those assumptions, but you make them anyway. If you found out that in fact while it looked really dreamy from where you are standing, that the boat didn't have a motor, and there was a giant hole in the hull on the other side of the boat, so it was sold dirt cheap at a repossession auction, then you would probably feel a bit silly. Another scenario is the boat was left to the neighbor by his recently deceased father and the neighbor was trying to sell it to someone else because it brings up so many painful memories about his father. I would imagine that you would feel quite embarrassed (and hopeful that you might be able to buy the boat yourself).

But this is just something our brains do. We make assumptions based on the idea that everybody else is luckier, smarter, better looking or more astute with money matters than ourselves. Yet the assumptions we make are not founded around any framework of facts! It is almost as though as a human race we like tricking ourselves into feeling inadequate. As individuals we don't have to have somebody else to make us feel bad, because we are really clever at doing it all by ourselves.

There is another thing we are good at – assuming that everybody else we know, who is out of the ordinary, famous, well-off or creative, has got some magic secret that makes them different to the ordinary person. Even if we had the inclination to do the things that famous people do (act, race cars, model, sing, lift weights, play sports, have rich parents) we would never assume that we could achieve the same level of success because rich and famous people are not ordinary people. *Famous people are not ordinary people? – what makes you think that?*

I learned a long time ago that so-called famous people are no different than you and me. They were born in the same way; they grew up in much the same way. They need to have air, food and water to live, just like us. They get themselves dressed in the same way as we do, pulling their pants on one foot at a time. In fact, there is nothing that a famous person does that is any different to the things you and I do everyday: it's just that more people notice them due to the media attention. Think about it a minute and you will see that it is true.

Saying this, I don't want you to stop for a moment and think that it is not worth being successful, even famous, because of course it is. But what you need to understand is that it is not a huge cavernous leap from where you are to where you want to be – mere mortals have been making that jump for centuries, and so can you.

A few years ago, a friend of mine confided that she had always wanted to be a writer just like J. K. Rowling, but she said "I would never be that good. J. K. Rowling is a legend among fiction writers. She has made more money than any other English writing fiction author in history. She's famous." I asked her why she thought she couldn't be as good a writer as her idol and she tried to explain that most writers don't make it in popular fiction; that her own career was papered with so many rejection slips she could paper a wall with them. She said J. K. Rowling must have something special because her own book was not only finished, it was published and she had gone on to write six more in the series.

I found the author's web site online and looked it over. It seems that J. K. Rowling had been writing since she was six years old. She had been working as a teacher when she had the idea of the Harry Potter series and she spent five years writing the first novel in time snatched from her other commitments of work and family life. The first Harry Potter book was written on the kitchen table, and was rejected by eight different publishers before it was finally accepted. I looked at my friend and said, "Well, you have a kitchen table don't you?"

The point of this story is to try and push home the idea that every famous person was ordinary once, unless born into a royal family and then they might be famous because of the family they were born into, but there are not that many royal families around. Even famous people get tired, have off days, feel depressed, get addicted to substances, catch the flu, and get pimples. Their feet stink if they don't change their socks, and they are just as capable of smelling up the bathroom as anybody else.

The only reason that my friend thought she couldn't become the next J. K. Rowling is because the gap between where my friend is now and where Ms. Rowling is now, appears to be quite a big one, but it is not insurmountable. There is no reason why, if my friend applies herself to her craft; is passionate about what she does and is persistent about getting her work published, that in a few years time she could be as rich and well known as Ms. Rowling is today. The same can be said of anyone else in pursuit of their dreams and passions. If you believe that you can achieve something, then half the battle is already won.

Although we can apply logic to assumptions we make to see how unfounded our thoughts can be, dealing with perception is that much harder, because every single person in the world has a different perception about any given situation at any given time. We touched on this topic briefly in the Introduction section and saw through example how our perception can impact all of our thoughts and behaviors. So where do our perceptions come from and why is it that even siblings can have different perceptions about the same event?

Our perceptions are as unique to us as our fingerprints. Because of the way we have been brought up, we all view situations and events differently.

Take a look at the summary table below:

Family Factors	Social Factors
Family unit type	Culture
Position in family (child order)	Ethnicity
Parenting styles	Rural/urban living
Family split ups – blended family	Neighborhood
Family dysfunction	Social interaction
Extended family	Schooling
Economic Factors	**Personal Factors**
Living standards	Personality type
Parents employment	Isolated/social
Leisure income	Learning or behavioral difficulties
Importance of money	Adaptable/flexible
Money spent on education	Emotional/mental stability

As you can see from the table above, the number of different combinations that could originate from these 22 elements is huge - and this list is in no way complete. For example, there are a multitude of different parenting types, cultural differences, forms of parental employment and learning and behavioral difficulties to name just a few. Throw in the impact of genetics and the list of possible combinations gets even bigger. So this list in itself can help illustrate why individual perceptions are so different, even within the same family.

Earlier in the Introduction section, we also discussed the way perceptions can change our thought processes, feelings, and then our behaviors. If you want to be successful, you need to understand how important the links are that exist between your thoughts, feelings and behaviors, and how perception provides the framework for all three of these things.

Actually, this link is probably more important than you are thinking even now – because we have only been talking about becoming successful up to this point. But, just as perceptions can help in your success, it is also a formidable barrier. Perceptions can impact you more than any other factor, element or variable in existence – it can sabotage your life given half the chance. It is possible, even as you read this, that this is something that has happened to you in the past already.

Sidney is a delightfully vivacious young woman, who is bright, smart, gets along with everybody and can turn her hand to anything. There is absolutely no reason whatsoever that she couldn't do whatever it is she wants. But in the past five years, Sidney has had over sixteen different jobs ranging from personal assistant in a large company, to manager of a coffee shop, to working with a peace activist movement, to waitressing in a local bar, to being an artist, making jewelry while working as a personal trainer, and so the list goes on.

Sidney's biggest problem is that people do like her, so she gets hired as a contractor for work easily enough. But then her bosses like her even more and offer her a permanent position, and it is around then that she usually gets sick. Physically sick. She goes to the doctor, they never know what is wrong with her and by the time she is feeling well enough to go back to work, she has been fired. Sidney's problem is that she never believed enough in herself to see that she was as good, if not better, at everything she did compared to anyone around her. She didn't believe that she had any work skills, people skills or any other talent that might be worth something on the job market, and when she came up with a good idea for self-employment - she sabotaged that as well. She always felt that she didn't add any skills or strengths to the team, when in fact, she was considered one of the strongest employees.

You see, perception works as the framework for everything we do, good or bad. Sidney's bright personality and her ease with people was just a façade, covering up a woman who had been abused as a child, a child that dealt with a parent addicted to substances and had thought of herself as worthless ever since. She expected to fail because she felt so bad about herself, and because of her perceptions about herself, she proved herself right every time. False perceptions were driving her life in the wrong direction.

Obviously, you don't have to be an abuse survivor to have negative perceptions about yourself. Many of us suffer from low self esteem (the most common by-product of negative perceptions about self) because of the things we have been told in our childhood and sometimes adulthood. When we were young, we might have been told not to try anything new by our overprotective parents. Or we might have been told to be "tough" and not cry by parents who could not handle any form of emotion. Even in really positive home environments a child picks up a form of social interaction that is copied from (or rebelling against) the way he or she has been brought up.

Then there are the perceptions that are formed because of external events; issues at school, natural disasters, news media, dating, growing up, learning to drive, getting a job, and going to college. If you think about it in the "wrong" way, life could be seen to be getting to you from the moment you are born. But for most of us, the impact of family in particular starts to wear off a bit after we have gone through college, moved out and away from home and found employment. These changes will affect the chances of us meeting somebody to share our lives with who is supportive, believes in our dreams and shares our passions. So the development of our perceptions lasts well beyond childhood and that is both good news and bad news for us as individuals.

The bad news is that if our perceptions are already negatively skewed, then you would think it would take an amazing and almost life changing event to put a positive slant on things. But the good news is that you can change your perceptions right now: within the next five minutes and honestly better your life. You might not believe this right now, but keep reading and you will see later in the book just how easy it is. But first, you need to understand what a complex beast we humans really are, because understanding is power.

The final point that needs to be made in this chapter is about how you feel about yourself. We have already illustrated how our perception of ourselves impacts our levels of success through the examples given, but now we need to concentrate on you specifically. There are over a million and one books written about how we should love ourselves, accept ourselves the way we are and treat ourselves a little better than most of us do, but sometimes the basics get lost in the details. So before I go any further in helping you create your dream life to be the success you want to be in a life of your choosing, I would like you to circle and fill out the following tests to see where you are right now.

There will be four tests on the following pages. It will be beneficial for you to complete all four tests so that you can get a better idea of what type of person you are right now. These results are not meant to be a form of judgement about you and there are no right or wrong answers. It's a good idea to see whereabouts on the playing field you are, before moving on to the work that will help you improve on your current score.

•

 www.stephenmark.com

First, something easy – let's see how happy you are. Just circle the response you feel most suits you to the five questions below.

How Happy Are You?

1. I feel my life is pretty good at this point in time						
Strongly Disagree	**Disagree**	**Slightly Disagree**	**Neutral**	**Slightly Agree**	**Agree**	**Strongly Agree**
1	2	3	4	5	6	7
2. I am happy with my home and work situation						
1	2	3	4	5	6	7
3. I feel good about myself and my life						
1	2	3	4	5	6	7
4. I am working on things that are important in my life						
1	2	3	4	5	6	7
5. I don't regret anything I have done so far in my life						
1	2	3	4	5	6	7

This is an easy test to score, simply add up the total of the numbers you have circled. Write your score down here _____. Now we can see briefly what these numbers mean.

If you scored **between 5 and 14**, this indicates you don't feel very happy in your life and you are probably living your life in accordance with other people, and you are not getting what you want in your life in any area including friendships, intimate relationships, work prospects, or leisure activities.

If you scored **between 15 – 25** you have your good moments. If your scored in this range, you should be able to identify some areas of your life that are making you happy, and through the process of elimination, be able to see areas of your life that need changing.

If you scored **between 26 – 31** you are, for the most part, a happy person. You obviously have a good sense of humor, like to go out and have some fun and you are more likely to view positive aspects about other people, rather than their negative traits. You can still increase your happiness, but all in all you are doing fine.

If you managed to get a score **between 31 and 35** you couldn't be any happier than you are right now. While that is really good in terms of enjoying your life and taking on new experiences, if you still don't feel you are very successful, then there must still be some area of your life that this brief test did not cover, or you are not admitting the problem to yourself.

We are going to leave any further analysis of this test until later in the chapter because there are a few other tests I would like you to take first, and then you will have a better understanding of the situation in your life as it is right now.

Ok, now we are going to look at your attitude and mood throughout the day.

This test is a little longer than the other one, there are thirty questions in all, but it is a good idea to answer them all so you can get a clear indication of how happy you are in practice on a day-to-day basis:

Attitude and Moods

1. I find something to laugh at in life everyday			
Strongly Disagree 1	2	3	**Strongly Agree** 4
2. I prefer people to be factual and unemotional when talking to me			
1	2	3	4
3. I often have sad days			
1	2	3	4
4. I find it easy to relax in positive surroundings			
1	2	3	4
5. I believe work comes before any leisure time			
1	2	3	4
6. I often feel irritable or bitter			
1	2	3	4

7. I find a silver lining in every cloud			
1	2	3	4

8. I consider myself an academic person			
1	2	3	4

9. I don't like it if I am being quiet and my friends insist on trying to make me feel better			
1	2	3	4

10. I am usually wearing a smile on my face			
1	2	3	4

11. I prefer to weigh things up carefully and write up lists of the pros and cons of any decision I have to make			
1	2	3	4

12. I do have bad days when I think I should have stayed in bed			
1	2	3	4

13. I am usually happy			
1	2	3	4

14. I search for the facts in a situation, and treat them seriously			
1	2	3	4

15. Sometimes I feel bad tempered for no apparent reason at all			
1	2	3	4

16. I find that laughter lifts my mood as well as others, so I laugh a lot			
1	2	3	4

17. I prefer serious conversations to people being silly			
1	2	3	4

18. Sometimes I can be in a good mood			
1	2	3	4

19. I feel at peace when surrounded by happy people			
1	2	3	4

20. I would rather watch serious programs like documentaries, than fun programs			
1	2	3	4

21. I have more "blue" days than good ones			
1	2	3	4

22. If other people laugh around me, I start laughing too			
1	2	3	4

23. I like to help other people or do chores when I have some spare time			
1	2	3	4

24. There are some days when I am so depressed nothing can bring me out of it			
1	2	3	4

25. I am basically a happy person			
1	2	3	4

26. I fill my days with important appointments and work commitments			
1	2	3	4

27. If someone is acting silly around me, they can put me in a bad mood			
1	2	3	4

28. I love making other people laugh			
1	2	3	4

29. I sometimes think my friends just want to have fun and nothing else			
1	2	3	4

30. Sometimes my "bad" days can last more than the one day			
1	2	3	4

How comfortable were you with completing this test? I realize that for some of you, actually admitting there might be more than a few days where you are not feeling so good could be hard for you to do. But you are only going to get success in life if you are truly honest with yourself. Nobody else needs to see your responses, so take the chance and trust the process.

Get to know the real you.

www.stephenmark.com

To score this test you need to complete the table on the next page. You will see that the test measures three different types of personality variables and that the questions you answered fall under one of three categories. To find out your score, simply write your numerical answer to each question in the table and then add up the columns. This will give you three separate scores concerning your attitudes and moods.

Being Happy		Being Serious		Being in a Bad Mood	
Question Number	Your Score	Question Number	Your Score	Question Number	Your Score
1		2		3	
4		5		6	
7		8		9	
10		11		12	
13		14		15	
16		17		18	
19		20		21	
22		23		24	
25		26		27	
28		29		30	
Your score		Your score		Your score	

Being Happy

If your score in the first column is **27 or less**, you are a very glum person. If you scored **between 28 and 30,** you could be considered gloomy as opposed to glum, but still not very happy. The issue with both of these scores is that you might have a tendency to hang on to petty concerns and problems. This can be a problem for two reasons: 1) the stress of carrying around the accumulated baggage you have could kill you and 2) the more petty worries you accumulate, the deeper the negative filter you view life through will become – which will result in more negativity.

Lighten up a bit and learn to let things go once in a while.

If you scored **between 31 and 34**, you could be called a glad person and if you **scored 35 to 37,** you could be considered bright and perky. If you have scored in either of these two ranges you are one of life's happier people, which is a really great way to be. You might not always be aware of problems around you and on the odd occasion you might hurt your friend if you tried to share your view of his or her problems with him or her, but basically you are a great person to be around, especially at a party.

If your score was **higher than 38,** Congratulations! You are a very happy person and you obviously take your life in stride. You are not as likely to be impacted by illness caused by stress and you have enough self esteem to keep you going through some of the most difficult situations life has to offer. Share your good humor with others.

Being Serious

This section was to find out if you thought things were funny (when they weren't) or if you have a more solemn outlook on life than people around you. If you scored **22 or less,** you consider most of the world is just too serious and you don't want to be a part of that. Just be careful that your love of pranks and jokes don't alienate you from your more serious friends.

If you scored *from* **23 to 27,** you do think about things quite seriously and you are not likely to join into silly things. You still have the capacity to have fun, which is a good thing, because if you scored in this range you are averagely serious which is a good balance to be.

If you scored **28 or more,** you are in a position where you just want life to be serious all the time and you have no time for any fun. People with this type of score are often workaholics, or spend all their time in academic pursuits. I am not suggesting for a minute that this is a bad thing, but you might want to try going out socially once in a while, or relaxing at the beach.

                    www.stephenmark.com

Being in a Bad Mood

This is the test that most people feel uncomfortable being honest with. None of us wants to be seen as controlling or irritable, or that we might have a temper problem. But honest acceptance of yourself can only occur through honest analysis, so if you think you might have fudged the test just a little bit, go back and change the scores to be a better reflection of who you are inside.

If you had a low score in this section of the test **16 or less,** you are the type of person who just doesn't let things get you down. You are usually in a good mood all of the time and you are able to handle any potential problems with a bit of tact and grace, which is a good thing. You are a very peaceful person to be around. If you score is a little higher, **between 17 and 21,** you are a pretty typical person. You do have some bad days, but not often and usually only when something particularly annoying or problematic springs up in your face.

If you scored **22 or higher** on this part of the test, you might want to think about changing your life, because it would appear that you have to struggle with every aspect of your life. The path through our lives is meant to have a few bumps in it, but we are not meant to fight so hard just to maintain the status quo. If you have scored highly here, this book will be helpful to you in terms of finding out the source of your bad mood and unhappiness, changing your life for the better.

The next test is designed to find out what type of event or experience you associate with the happiest times in your life. Some of the more common times we feel this way is if we have just witnessed the birth of a child, wedding days are another common high point in life, vacations, so to is graduating from college. Some of us get a lot of pleasure from taking a walk in a park or place of natural beauty, while the more physical among us may get the same pleasure from bungee jumping or white water rafting. Research has shown that there are nine "peak experience types"; that is experiences that we can have that will give us the most pleasure. These nine types of experiences are defined in the table below.

The Peak Experiences Test

The Nine Peak Experiences	
Peak Type	**Peak Experience Examples**
Social	Having fun with other people
Artistic	Enjoying or creating art, music or literary works
Athletic	Playing the game, excelling at what you do
Nature	Feeling a oneness with the power of nature
Sexual	The feeling of togetherness that comes from intimacy
Altruistic	The high you get when you help other people
Chemical	The high you can get from drugs
Academic	The pleasure that can come from learning
Political	The excitement that comes from putting your ideas into action

This test format is true and false statements. Statement starters are listed at the top of two columns. Statement endings are listed below. Make sure you read the top of the column before you read the statement below it. Then answer "True" or "False" as to whether or not that full statement applies to you. Once again, remember there are no right or wrong answers here; you are just trying to understand what type of experiences you have had through your life.

I <u>have had</u> an experience that made me extremely happy, and at least temporarily...		I <u>have never</u> had an experience that made me extremely happy and at least temporarily...	
1. Made me feel more unique than I usually feel	T/F	2. Removed much of my perplexity and confusion	T/F
3. Caused me to feel that the world was sacred	T/F	4. Moved me closer to a perfect identity	T/F
5. Caused my private, selfish concerns to fade away	T/F	6. Helped me to totally accept the world	T/F
7. Gave my whole life new meaning	T/F	8. Made me want to do something good for the world	T/F
9. Caused time to seem to stand still	T/F	10. Made me feel very lucky and fortunate	T/F
11. Caused me to feel great kindness towards humanity	T/F	12. Made me feel as if all my wants and needs were satisfied	T/F
13. Caused me to like and accept everyone	T/F	14. Allowed me to realize that everyone has his/her place in the universe	T/F
15. Caused me to feel that the world is totally good	T/F	16. Made me accepting of pain that I usually am in	T/F
17. Caused me to become disorientated in time	T/F	18. Made me feel both proud and humble at the same time	T/F
19. Removed many of my inhibitions	T/F	20. Gave me a sense of obligation to do constructive things	T/F

I <u>have had</u> an experience that made me extremely happy, and at least temporarily…		I <u>have never</u> had an experience that made me extremely happy and at least temporarily…	
21. Made me feel freer than I usually feel	T/F	22. Involved total listening	T/F
23. Made me very grateful for the privilege of having had it	T/F	24. Gave my life new worth	T/F
25. Made me feel as if I had everything, I could not think of anything else that I wanted	T/F	26. Caused me to feel that the world is totally beautiful	T/F
27. Reduced my anxiety level greatly	T/F	28. Helped me to appreciate beauty to a greater degree than I usually do	T/F
29. Caused me to believe that I could not be disappointed by anyone	T/F	30. Put me in a state of total concentration	T/F
31. Gave me great insight	T/F	32. Led me to realize that there is meaningfulness to the universe	T/F
33. Caused me to feel that people are sacred	T/F	34. Caused me to view the world as totally desirable	T/F
35. Led me to accept everything	T/F	36. Made the conflicts of life seem to disappear	T/F
37. Caused me to become disorientated in space	T/F	38. Helped me to a greater appreciation of perfection	T/F
39. Helped me to realize that I could never commit suicide	T/F	40. Led me to believe that I could die with dignity	T/F

Now bearing in mind again that there are no right or wrong answers, the scoring of this test is done against a set of answers provided. Match your answers to the table on the next page and score yourself one point for each matching answer.

(circle each matching answer)

1	2	3	4	5	6	7	8	9	10
T	F	T	F	T	F	T	F	T	F
11	12	13	14	15	16	17	18	19	20
T	F	T	F	T	F	T	F	T	F
21	22	23	24	25	26	27	28	29	30
T	F	T	F	T	F	T	F	T	F
31	32	33	34	35	36	37	38	39	40
T	F	T	F	T	F	T	F	T	F

Your Score _____

This is one of the few tests included in this book that is gender impacted, but of course most men and women do tend to view pleasure, happiness and unhappiness in different ways so it is logical that a peak experience test result would vary depending on your gender.

For Women 27 or less: Men 26 or less

If you scored **27 or less** in this test, you are not the type of person to enjoy any form of peak experience. It sounds like you are a very grounded person, which in itself is not a bad thing, but you are denying yourself some real joy if you don't take the time to enjoy some happy experiences to the fullest.

Women 28 – 32: Men 27 – 31

If you scored **between 28 and 32,** you have had the occasional peak experience and you seem to have a balanced life that sits between following rules and following your heart. This is a really healthy way to be, and you should find a successful life just around the corner, if you haven't stumbled on it already.

Women 33 or more: Men 32 or more

If you *scored* **32 or more,** you are a really creative person who has found a fine balance between being tolerant and caring and also assertive where necessary. Your peak experiences come from your ability to live in the moment when appropriate and you also have the skills to succeed in life.

Do You Sabotage Your Success?

This last test is slightly different in that it deals with the concepts of self-sabotage. This is something we have touched on briefly in this book with our story on Sidney, and we will be looking at this problem in later chapters. For now, the test will help you to identify if you are the type of person to sabotage your own success and if you are prone to sabotaging things at the last minute, and what type of sabotage techniques you use.

This is a multiple-choice test – pick one response to each question.

(Remember no one is grading you – this is for you)

1. If you were in debt, it would likely be because
   A) You have a lavish lifestyle
   B) You pay for other people's fun and entertainment
   C) You like to enjoy yourself
   D) You are just not very good at managing money

2. You are not likely to get a promotion at work because
   A) The timing is just not right for you
   B) You are already overworked
   C) You are not interested in extra responsibility
   D) Promotions are for high flyers

3. You are most likely to fight with your partner because
   A) They don't see things your way
   B) They treat you like a doormat
   C) You don't have fun anymore
   D) You often say the wrong thing

4. Your motto would be
   A) Higher, faster and stronger
   B) Give an inch, they take a mile
   C) Live for today
   D) If it ain't broke, don't fix it

5. You are more likely to miss a proposal deadline because
    A) There isn't enough time to do the job properly
    B) You were struggling and no one offered to help you
    C) You got caught up doing other things more interesting
    D) You don't feel the work you have done is worthwhile

6. Hosting a dinner party, you are more likely to overcook the meal because
    A) Guests don't arrive on time
    B) No one offers to help
    C) You are too busy enjoying yourself to notice the time
    D) Your dinner parties are usually a disaster anyway

7. You would rather be
    A) Perfect
    B) Strong
    C) Free
    D) Acceptable

8. You are more likely to drink too much at the office party because you
    A) Can normally hold your drink
    B) Can't say no when someone tops up your glass
    C) Like to have a good time
    D) Have always been a lightweight

9. You are more likely to have a bad time while on holiday because
    A) The resort didn't live up to expectations
    B) It's hard to have fun when you are left to organize everything
    C) It isn't in the stars
    D) You can't let yourself relax and let go

10. You are more likely to be remembered for
    A) Doing it all
    B) Being generous to a fault
    C) Living large
    D) Your modesty

                www.stephenmark.com

To tally up your score for this test, work out how many "A", "B", "C" or "D" answers you have and which letter you scored the most in.

If you have mostly "A" answers, you are known as a "perfectionist" who is really quite worried about being found out as a bit of a fraud. Your thinking is the "all or nothing" party line and this is not getting you anywhere. Your good enough probably is good enough if you just let it be.

If you have mostly "B" answers, you are like a "pendulum". You have a lot of problems because you are unsure of yourself and don't know how to set boundaries that other people will respect. You will find your mood alternates from being angry to feeling resentful, and you probably feel a bit like the doormat. Your problems can be helped by writing a personal charter and in a journal (later in the book).

If you have mostly "C" answers, you reflect the "connoisseur" of worrying. You are so worried that you might not succeed that you decide to avoid any form of responsibility completely. You would benefit from deciding which goals are important to you and construct a plan to make it happen.

The "D" responders are fairly self-evident. This is a person who has very low self-esteem and always thinks that anything around them that might be wrong is probably their fault. You need to focus on your strengths and to appreciate the achievements you have everyday. Believe it or not, getting out of bed in the morning is an achievement not all of us can master, so write that on your list and add anything else to the list that will make you feel better about yourself.

That's it for the testing in this chapter. You may be feeling a bit bewildered or even overwhelmed at this point, because the mere act of answering questions about yourself sends you on a journey of self-discovery. At this stage, just fill in the table on the opposite page with your final answers for all of this work, as we will refer back to it later on.

If you are feeling a bit uncomfortable, remember that in a situation where you can make changes in your life, or choose not to, that it is your choice and your actions that actually propel your life along the path that you have chosen.

Some of you may feel even worse when you consider that maybe your actions or thoughts in the past might be responsible for current misfortunes, but this is not a blame game, this is the game of cause and effect. For now go and make yourself a cup of hot tea or coffee; sit down somewhere quiet, warm and comfortable, and just let your mind roam freely.

Remind yourself that you are the skipper of your life, that you have every reason to love and accept yourself, because you are a unique and wonderful human being.

Test Taken	**Your Score**
1. How happy are you?	Number Score _____
2. Attitude and Moods – Happy score	Number Score_____
3. Attitude and Moods – Serious score	Number Score_____
4. Attitude and Moods – Bad mood	Number Score_____
5. Nine peak experiences	Number Score _____
6. Self Sabotage – Mostly ____(Letter) that indicates _____ (Sabotage type).	

                                            www.stephenmark.com

Chapter Two

How Do We Measure Success Anyway?

Heather is standing at her kitchen sink washing dishes. In fact, she is staring out across the yard lost in a world of her own. Behind her, the three children are arguing over what to have for breakfast, before her husband came running in, grabbed a cup of coffee off the breakfast table, kissed her distractedly on the cheek and muttered something about being late as he took off to work. The three kids are alerted that the bus is at the door so they take off yelling things for their mom to remember to buy that day and Heather is left alone in the silence that comes immediately following all the chaos. She gives herself a shake as if to remind herself where she is and she turns to view the carnage on the breakfast table. "There must be more to life than this," she mutters to herself as she gets a cloth and starts cleaning up.

There are over a million women like Heather who seem lost in a dream world as they go about their day. They are dreaming as a form of escapism from the banal elements of their lives. Lives of their own choosing it should be noted, but banal lives just the same. These women (and some men) have been caught up in a specific life plan from their early adult years, and then somehow or other they got caught up in the day to day tasks and the dreams they had as they were growing up became nothing more than distant memories. One day they wake up and look in the mirror and all of a sudden they don't recognize the person staring back at them: where did their lives and passions go?

It is really easy to get caught up in the business of living. We leave college and go out into the workforce. Once there, we get caught up in the whole idea of consumerism – we buy things. Lots of things. Things we probably don't need, but we get them anyway. Once those small things like new clothes start to merge into higher priced items like furniture, we start looking at higher purchase and credit options to get the things we think we need and the spending doesn't stop there. Next stop, buying a house to put all this stuff in. Then what happens? We have children (and don't let anybody tell you they are not expensive) and then before you know it, you are staring middle age in the face and your dramatic and passionate life has mysteriously morphed into rut from which there seems to be no escape. Your own children are talking about going to college and you see yourself buried under a mountain of debt and commitments for so far into the future, you forget to dream because you feel there is just no point. So, do you think this a successful life?

For many of us, this type of scenario is our lives, and so yes, we do think we are relatively successful. Face it, we conduct our lives in an ever-changing playing field. Job security is no longer guaranteed; employment is merit or target based; finance companies are failing due to a changing global economy, interests rates rise while incomes falls. To be gainfully employed at a level that benefits your level of education is a bonus, as is being able to afford your mortgage and still have a comfortable life. It's ironic really because in many cases we still measure our successes on the same basis as our parents and grandparents did, yet the world in which we live is totally different. But as long as we are employed, can get credit, ensure our children grow up in a relatively stable environment and have plans for our retirement, many of us think of ourselves as successful. But are we really?

It was Dr. Phil McGraw, a popular visitor on the Oprah Winfrey Show and who now has his own show on the Harpo network, that first talked

  www.stephenmark.com

publicly to the masses about the measures of success. While many life coaches and motivators had run personalized programs targeted to meet specific target audiences, it was Dr. Phil (as he is known) who kept reiterating that everybody could be a success and that success was not dependent on how much money a household had. Nor was success based on the position a person held in his or her working life, or what colleges his or her children attended. No, Dr. Phil was concerned about the measures of success that ensured that an individual, or family were happy.

Being happy has been the topic of literally hundreds of self-help books, but the strange thing is that happiness itself cannot be accurately measured. After all, we are all different and so we view the events and situations happening in our lives differently than other people do. A hermit living in a cave in the Himalayas could consider himself happy and yet in our society today he would be deemed homeless, possibly strange, and a drop out. A CEO of a large company could kid himself that he is happy every time he gets paid, but the hours spent away from his wife and children can be considered by some to be too high a price to pay for that sense of worth.

Our standard of living is a relative term as well, yet many people assume that they will be considered successful if they attain certain standards – usually those set by neighbors, friends, or families. Our society now has such huge divides between the "haves" and the "have nots" that the people of higher monetary worth are automatically deemed as successful, and because their standard of living is so high, many people in the lower socio-economic groups (which make up the majority) think that the monetary gap is too large to bridge, so they become automatically unsuccessful. What most "ordinary people" don't realize is that many people on the fringes of monetary wealth are often sustaining their position in their well-off society through a high use and abuse of numerous credit resources.

Some studies in early 2000 showed that many people considered successful and on a high income are so badgered by credit card and other forms of personal debt that they could only survive a few weeks without a paycheck, or face bankruptcy. This is because the amount of interest that is charged on so many credit lines is so high, that a large monthly income is required just to pay off the minimum due payment each month. If we assume that it is not money that is the measure of success, but say happiness at home instead, then it is highly possible that very few of the wealthy people among us are actually successful. Sound familiar?

Remember the story about J. K. Rowling that I discussed in the first chapter of this book and how my writer friend was so sure she could never reach the same level of success as her idol, Ms. Rowling? I described how Ms. Rowling wrote her first Harry Potter book from her kitchen table, snatching moments when she could because of her busy family life. She had to earn a living and she had a household to run, but what made her successful is that she had an idea **she believed in and she persevered with it**. Now she is a household name in so many countries around the world, even she has probably lost count.

Another famous person who came from a very poor and abusive childhood is Oprah Winfrey. She has never been shy about discussing the poverty that was evident in her life until she left home in her mid-teens, and the abuse she suffered has also been recorded in a number of interviews. Oprah credits her success to her extremely strong belief in herself. She won a beauty pageant to get noticed for television, and it was during her stint as a reporter that she was offered first an anchor position and then her own talk show. Bearing in mind this was more than a few years ago, her quick rise to television talk show host was surprisingly fast given she was both female and an African American. She credits part of her success to her hard work ethics, instilled by her father. Oprah also credits her grandmother, who taught Oprah to read when she was just 3 years old, as being a strong female role model.

Oprah Winfrey is a success on so many levels. She is touted as the first and currently only African American woman billionaire. She owns a number of companies under her Harpo umbrella. She has maintained a solid relationship with her live-in partner; has numerous friends and has created charity networks all over the United States and in many parts of Africa. Ultimately though, Oprah Winfrey is happy because she is doing what she loves – talking to people. She was recently quoted as saying "It doesn't matter who you are [or] where you come from. The ability to triumph begins with you. Always". She has been a living example of that belief for more than fifty years.

There are quite literally hundreds of examples in our world of people who have become successful in the socially accepted sense of the word, despite poor or impoverished beginnings. These people have made a difference in their world and in ours – look at the legacy of people like Mother Theresa, Mahatma Gandhi, and Anita Roddick who founded the Body Shop in 1976 from her garage in England.

The Body Shop has become a major international corporation that provides a range of cosmetic and beauty products that are all guaranteed free from animal testing or any other practice that went against the company's strong environmental responsibility policy. The network has since been active in a number of environmental causes since the late 1980's.

So how do you measure your own success? Is it remotely possible that you are already a success and just don't appreciate it? That is possible you know. If your measure of success is based on providing your children with special memories of their childhood when they are old, and you spend a lot of time with your children, then it is likely you would consider that a success even though you will not really get any personal benefit from your children's future memories. After all, if you are at your happiest when you spend time with your children, then it is likely you would consider yourself a success if you can do this regularly.

Many men consider their success is measured in the size of their bank accounts or their physical prowess. Women are geared in a slightly different way and may consider their personal relationships or their ability to be creative as the key to whether or not they are successful. What about you? How did you score in the happiness test (Chapter one) for example?

If you recall, in the happiness test your scores were evaluated from below 27 to above 38. If you scored below 27, you were considered a particularly glum type of person, while if you scored higher than 38, you belonged in the bright and perky group. Now ask yourself, would you have scored in this test differently if you measured your success in terms other than money or belongings? It is worth thinking about.

I want you to start creating a gratitude list. Actually two lists; it can be ten items long or twenty; the number of items is not important. What is important is the content of this list. I want you to write down every single thing you have in your life to be happy about – things you can be grateful for. This is not an exercise you can do in five minutes. Actually, it would be better if you took a half day away from your commitments, and spent some quiet time alone thinking about your life and how you feel about the people, the situations and the events of your life. I am sure you will be surprisingly pleased about the number of things you have to be grateful for. To help you get started I have listed part of a gratitude list. The full list could have had over a hundred items on it. Make it a point of adding one thing to it at least three times per week. The more you focus on the things you are grateful for, the better your life will become and will enable you to help others.

Gratitude List

I am grateful for...	The reason I am grateful is...
I woke up feeling good this morning	I never take my life for granted
I was able to get out of bed this morning	I never take my physical health for granted
I feel good and pain free this morning	There have been many mornings when I woke to severe migraines
I have a healthy wife	I don't take my family life for granted, or my families health. In the horror stories we hear everyday on the news, I am pleased that everyone in my life is doing well today
I have healthy and happy children / parents / pets / friends / family	

I am grateful for...	The reason I am grateful is...
I have the benefit of an education so I can work from home	So many people are locked into work conditions that drain them of their life's energy. I value the fact that I can work from home and I have control over what I do in my day
I have the tools I need to work from home	
I can go outside and enjoy the sun, the fresh air and my lifestyle in absolute safety	Like the reasons given above, I never lose site of the fact that I am really lucky because I live in a place where my health is not compromised by technology, but rather enhanced by it, and we have the staples of life
We have food in the refrigerator and cupboard	
I have goals to pursue with the means to pursue them	Everyone needs something to work towards in their life – I am hoping to spend time on creative pursuits in the near future
I am supported emotionally and spiritually by my family	Although I enjoy my own company, I love the support network that has evolved around me over the years
I am so aware and thankful for every day as a special gift	I have faced death many times, and while I don't fear death, I still appreciate every day I am alive

Do you remember earlier in this book we talked about how **our perceptions impact our actions?** How many people stopped themselves from succeeding because they believed that they needed money first to make money? Hopefully this is one myth you have happily dispelled from your life. Gratitude and being thankful is something you can use to build other successes on. When we work from a place of empowerment, from gratitude, peace and calm in our inner selves, we remain more firmly connected to the Universe, more focused on our path and more good things come into our lives – the Law of Attraction guarantees it.

There is one more exercise I want you to do before we move on and that is to **write out a list of your priorities.** Take some time and work out what things in your life are worth hanging on to and what things – like emotional baggage, hate, envy, anger or hurt - you have learned enough from and are ready to let go of. Use the blank space below to make a list.

Chapter Three

Who Is Running Your Life?

In today's hectic world it is easy to feel like your life is running you, and you're just along for the ride. Maybe you work full-time outside of the home, have a family, a mortgage, car or student loans. There are meetings to attend, carpools to drive, places to be, you're an important person, people are counting on you. Does it ever feel like there are too many things to do, and not enough hours in the day? Do you struggle for the balance between what you have to do, and what you want to do?

In a constant state of stress, we often feel disorganized and drained. There are things you can do to eliminate the things that are draining your time and zapping your energy. Getting it touch with your goals and motivations will help you to focus your intention and create a healthier balance in your life.

Let's start by focusing a little on time itself. Most everyone is busy, but when asked "doing what?" the answers come slower. How are you spending your time? Are you aware of where your time goes? How much of your time is really yours? Let's take a look.

Start this exercise by focusing on the key areas of your life. For example, you may identify the following as major components:

- Professional/Work
- Family
- Relationships
- Hobbies
- Relaxation
- Faith/Spirituality

Prepare a list using the above or create your own. Next, assign a percentage to every area, representing the amount of time you spend on each in a given month. (When tallying the percentages they should reach 100%).

Life Component	Percentage of Time Spent
1. Professional/Work	%
2. Family	%
3. Relationships	%
4. Hobbies	%
5. Relaxation	%
5. Faith/Spirituality	%
Total Percentage of Time Spent	100 %

How much time do you devote to each area on a weekly basis? What about daily? Are there days when some areas get 0%? When reviewing your percentages, I'm sure you'll find you'd like to spend more time in some areas and less in others. Keep in mind this is what your life looks like now. Begin to imagine how you'd like it to look. Remember, with some work you can create a different picture!

Buddha said, "The trouble is that you think you have time." Many of us will pack our already busy schedules so full of activities that if we actually accomplished everything, we'd wear capes and be known as superheroes. Feeling busy can be satisfying, but it can also leave us scattered. While finding time is difficult, making the time you spend meaningful is not.

You should think about completing or changing anything that drains your energy in a negative way. Those can be the 25 little things that nag at you, in the back of your brain all the time. You know the loose wood plank on the front steps? That squeaking sounds your car makes when you start your engine? What about the loose floor tiles in the kitchen? Make a list, that's right, a list of everything that's bothering you. Your list might include 10 things; it might reach 100 or more. The reason you're going to write down these annoyances is because you're going to feel a release as you deal with each item and cross it off the list. Devote an hour a day or a week, and tackle these little things that have been on your mind. These things drain your energy because they are annoying you. Make your list, get to work, and cross the drains off. You'll experience more energy as your list gets smaller.

Back when you did the time percentage exercise, you identified areas of importance in your life. Who are the important people in your life? What roles do they play in the decisions you make about how you spend your time, how you spend your money, where you live, where you work, what you do for fun? How much influence do your relationships have on the choices you make for yourself? In what ways do they impact your life?

Are you consciously making decisions about your life on a daily basis? Not just how you spend your time, and who you spend it with, but what are you doing to create the life you want? World famous motivational speaker, Tony Robbins once said, "How am I going to live today in order to create the tomorrow I'm committed to?" That is the challenge isn't it?

Take a moment to reflect on the important people in your life. Who are they, and what roles do they play in your life? Think about the different roles you yourself play. For instance, if you work, you play the role of employee or even boss. If you have a husband or wife, you play the role of spouse, if you have children, you play the role of parent, and so on. We are all many things at once and balance our different roles.

Identify the major players in your life in the following table.

Name – Their Role in Your Life	Your Role in Their Life
Name	*Role*
Name	*Role*
Name	*Role*
Name	*Role*
Name	*Role*
Name	*Role*

Now, reflecting on the relationships above, **how much** of an impact do they have on your day-to-day decisions? Do you find yourself trying to please them? **Why** are you trying to please them? **What** if you do please them? **How** will that change your life? **What does your life feel like when you don't please them?**

Generally **we all want to be loved and accepted by other people.** Are your actions motivated by your desires or the perceived desires of others? Do you think people will only love you if you do things to please them? For example, if you say:

> **"I want everyone to be happy."** This is extremely general.

> **"Who do you want to be happy?"** and

"How will you know they are happy?" and

"If they express to you they are happy,

how will this impact you?"

A friend of mine named Tiffany wanted to land a job she had found in the local classified ads. It was more prestigious than her current position, and the wages were much higher. "My parents will be so proud of me if I get this job," she told me. I asked why it would make her parents happy. She said it would illustrate that Tiffany was putting all her college and Mastery training to use and would prove that Tiffany was smart.

WOW!

Talk about being motivated by someone other than herself. I encouraged Tiffany to explore her motivations.

Let's look at it from some different perspectives:

- What would happen if her parents believed she was utilizing all her University and Mastery training?

- Would this belief impact her relationship with her parents?

- Would her parents love her more if she believed it to be true?

- Was validation from her parents motivating Tiffany to apply for a job, when Tiffany found satisfaction in her current position at a less prestigious firm?

- What would happen if she didn't get the job?

- And what if she did get the job, and nothing between her and her parents changed? What then?

Of course our families play roles in our perceptions about life. Families of origin shape our visions and beliefs about ourselves and the outside world. Tiffany felt responsible to prove to her parents that she was smart and that she could achieve a prestigious position, even though she was quite happy with her current job.

If you grew up in a family, you were undoubtedly exposed to dysfunction in some shape or form. If you've been alive for very long, you've experienced disappointment at some level personally or professionally. You've been hurt, disappointed, angry, lied to, and disillusioned on at least one occasion. Admit it. However, it is up to you how you allow your past experiences to shape your present and your future. Every experience allows you to learn and create. To create the life you want, you have to appreciate the good things in your life and begin **creating from a place of gratitude and abundance.**

You can still acknowledge the feelings of disappointment, but it's important that you **stop the negative** tape that plays in the back of your mind. Negative experiences have created the tape, and it's up to you to consciously change the tape and replace it with positive experiences. Stop looking for what's wrong and start saying thank you.

Sometimes we generalize or make assumptions about situations. This is self-sabotaging behavior. We deal with our disappointments in this manner, and sometimes we make excuses for things not going our way. Doing so does not allow us to learn from the situation or to allow all the possibilities that the situation holds to present themselves. Some examples of generalizing might be:

"He must be angry with me because he didn't call me."
You're assuming he's angry because he didn't call you.

"If she doesn't start paying the bills, they will kick her out."
Did they tell you they are going to ask her to leave?

"She didn't send me a postcard, I guess she didn't miss me."
You're making assumptions about your friend's feelings.

"I didn't hear back about that job. I must have really blown the interview."
You're making assumptions about your own performance.

"If she really liked me, she would have invited me to the party."
You're making assumptions about your friend's feelings.

It's important to keep in mind that **we can learn and grow from every experience.** Our perception of our experiences are what need to be shifted before we can create more bountiful lives. By generalizing, we make assumptions about things and we take it very personally. We illustrated this in an earlier part of the book. There are always other factors at work that we don't know about, and when we make assumptions, well you've heard the old saying about making an ass out of yourself.

When we set goals, we're creating a game plan for our life. Maybe the goals are things that can be easily achieved, like cleaning the garage. A few hours on a weekend and you can scratch that goal off the list – you achieved it. Other more intense goals might take longer, like finding a new job, or new home, or new partner. Before committing to goals for things you want in your life, take a few moments to appreciate what you already have. It's important to create from a place of satisfaction, or your goal list suddenly has 100 items on it, most of them seeming out of reach. You can't do much of anything if you're feeling overcome with frustration. *Right?*

Journaling can be a powerful tool in creating the life you want. I encourage you to spend the next few weeks starting a daily journal entry with the following:

"I am so grateful for the abundance of gifts I have in my life..." and then you list them. Use the list you made at the end of Chapter Two as the framework for this. This journal exercise is a way of building on the positive things in your life. The laws of attraction are always at work, even as you are reading and learning. What you focus on, is what you attract to yourself. If you focus on what you are lacking, your feeling of lacking will continue. **Journal entries are important because you write about what you want your life to look like. You write about it as though it is currently happening.**

A journal entry may look something like this, keeping in mind, it's YOUR life that you are creating:

"I am so grateful for the abundance of gifts I have in my life. I enjoy a challenging and rewarding career, loving and healthy relationships, financial abundance, and excellent health."

You describe your life as you want it to be, and your perceptions about your life will slowly shift. Not only will you feel more content with your life after a couple of weeks, you'll begin attracting things that will allow you to achieve the abundance you'be been writing about. Journaling allows you to focus on what you want.

If you have a wish list of what you want to accomplish, take a moment to think the list over. What is your motivation for undertaking these challenges? Are they things you want for yourself? Or do you want it for someone else? Will it better your life? Will it better someone else's life? Will it make someone else happy with you? Is it important to you that you consider the feelings of others before taking action? How will you feel when you reach these goals?

Here are some examples of what I mean:

"When I buy that new car, that's when she'll notice me."
What happens if you buy the car, and she doesn't notice you?

(Are you not the same person, regardless of the vehicle you drive? What if she does notice you? How will that change your life?)

"If I were skinnier, he'd be attracted to me."
What if you became skinnier, and he's not attracted to you?

(What if you changed your size and he did notice you? Are you seeking approval from others or are you interested in changing for yourself? What will change in your life if he does notice you?)

"I'd really like my boss to raise my wages."
How will you feel if he doesn't?

(Is your validation tied to your compensation? Will getting an increase in wages change your job or your position in the company?)

I would encourage you to run things through the **cause and effect test**. Are you motivated by the concept of "if this happens, then that will happen" as illustrated above? Have you considered why you want the things you do? Be clear on your motivations.

Do you envision your goals, what you'll feel like when you've achieved them? Do you try to mirror yourself after someone who you know that has been successful? Are you motivated by success, a feeling of accomplishment, a feeling of pride? With an already busy schedule, how do you decide what you're going to accomplish each day? What about for the week? Do you set goals for yourself each month? When we go to work, our organization typically sets our goals for us. What about in our personal lives? It's your responsibility to set your own life goals – keeping in mind, these can change over time as you find your true passion. **Create a list of personal life goals before moving on.**

You've identified what activities you're spending time doing. You've also identified the important players in your life. Your motivations could be external or internal. Hopefully you've created a list of goals you want to accomplish. You've created your list when in a state of satisfaction, not frustration. Now you need to create the roadmap to getting there.

What do you perceive are the roadblocks to achieving your goals? Can you imagine what's standing in your way? Some roadblocks will be real, others imagined. Self-doubt can creep in and make us lose focus and even worse, bring fear into our lives. So I want you to take your list and create two columns next to each goal. You're going to identify the possible obstacles or things that might distract you, and also how you will attack the challenges. For example:

Goal	Possible obstacles	Plan of Attack
Lose 10 lbs	I don't enjoy exercise	Daily walks around the block
	I enjoy food	Read labels, make healthy choices
Buy a new car	Expensive	Set aside 5% of each paycheck

The "Plan of Attack" column is important, because it affirms your commitment to the goal and illustrates steps you can take to achieve your goal. **Instead of focusing on why you can't, your list will focus on ways you can.** The next step is to create a realistic timeline or deadline. An open-ended goal, with no end date is something that is easy to procrastinate. Let's discuss for a moment the perils of procrastination and why we do it.

First, a big reason people procrastinate is because they don't want to do the task. Well, if you don't want to do it, you probably shouldn't be doing it! How will you achieve contentment if you're not doing things that enhance your life? If you don't want to do something, you will spend a lot of energy finding ways to avoid it. Energy that you could be applying elsewhere.

Maybe you procrastinate because you don't know where to start? Ask someone! Another person may be able to give you the information you need to get going. Another good friend of mine always wanted to travel through Africa. Her love of history, architecture and wildlife suggested that she'd enjoy visiting Egypt and South Africa. Her goal was clear, but she had no idea how much the trip would cost, how long it would take, and she just knew her boss would never allow her so much time off, and she doubted she'd be able to afford the trip at all. So one day I asked her if she'd contacted any travel agencies. Did she know how long her dream trip would actually take? Had she any idea what it would cost? My friend was so sure she couldn't get the time off and sure she'd not be able to afford the journey, she had taken no action to make her trip a reality. If you're not creating forward momentum, you're moving backwards.

A simple phone call provided all the information she needed. It turned out the travel company she contacted offered 10 day tours, and her employer granted her 14 vacation days for the year. The cost of the trip was also half of what she had imagined! All of the sudden, the trip she thought was impossible, was a possibility because she armed herself with information.

A common reason for procrastination is because you're convinced you just don't have the time. Let's revisit the concept of time. One technique that's proved effective in finding time where you think there isn't time is to spend a week tracking your time, that's right, every hour make a note of how you've spent your time. Track the time during a normal week that involves your typical routine and tasks. At the end of the week you will have a record of the things you've been doing that a) only you can do and b) that can be delegated to others. You'll also notice time-wasters on your list. How many hours are spent in front of the television set? How about time spent checking voicemail? How about reading and responding to emails, trying to delete all the spam? You can't manage what you can't see. *Right?*

What would happen if you decided to set your morning alarm 12 minutes earlier? At the end of the working week you'd have an extra hour. Drinking your morning coffee in your own kitchen instead of hitting the local hot java spot on the way to work, you could save nearly another hour each week, plus the financial savings that come with that. During the working day, what would happen if you dealt with emails the first 10 minutes of each hour, instead of constantly being interrupted throughout the day? Could you retrieve voicemails once each hour as well? You'll be interrupted throughout the day by co-workers, but could you reduce the interruptions by closing your door, or posting a notice that alerted them you're working on an important project? Can you limit your meetings to mornings only, or schedule working luncheons? Could you schedule weekly meetings with your boss or subordinates to cover non-emergency issues, rather than checking-in several times each day? How much time do you think you could save?

Ask yourself every morning just what is important about today; what has to get done today; and what is important about the future? These questions require that you prioritize and that you plan. Prioritize the most important things first, keeping in mind what's coming up. Rather than managing time, think of it as managing your tasks. Have you ever done this? Most of us have not.

If you are able to de-clutter your workspace, you will find it much easier to focus on the tasks that you determine are top priority. There are different methods for handling clutter, and a tried and true rule is generally if you haven't touched a piece of paper in a month, it doesn't belong on your desk. Maybe it should be filed in your cabinet, or recycled. Invest the time you need to make your workspace a place devoid of chaos and trade it in for a place of serenity.

Begin your day by jotting down what MUST get done before the day is over. Schedule your day around getting the important stuff accomplished. If this means you have to implement a "do not disturb" rule outside your office, do it. If it means your phone calls have to go to voicemail, do it.

Another thing we do to save time is multi-task. The concept of multi-tasking is flawed in many ways. We can only do one thing at a time, literally. Multi-tasking isn't efficient, because you're not focused on any one thing. I encourage you to do your tasks, just one thing at a time. The truth is, that is all you can do. Beginning today, STOP one activity before you START the next. All that ever comes out of chaos is chaos. Just like all the people telling you to think outside of the box, you become less focused on what you are doing and trying to accomplish.

When you are more focused on a specific topic or goal, it can be brought to fruition if thinking in the box. So be sure to watch where you focus your energies.

When you track your time and see how much time you're devoting to things, you can determine what you want to spend your time on. Are you doing the things that bring you joy? Are you living the life you want to live? If you reduce your interruptions and eliminate time-wasters, you're in control.

With just two extra hours each week, you can devote energy to things that bring you fulfillment, fun, and enjoyment. Perhaps more time with your children or spouse or some much needed time for meditation or special interests. Turn off that television and go for a walk, read a book, play with the children or have a special date with your spouse or significant other. Track, analyze, and decide how you'll spend your time, and who with. If a business were not to plan, analyze, focus, and just do everyday, where do you think they will end up? We are no different.

Another obstacle you may experience when you begin taking charge of your life is the issue of boundaries. Boundaries are essential to having healthy professional and personal relationships. They are the lines that are not okay for anyone to cross, and they offer you protection. A boundary example could be it's not okay for someone to physically touch or assault you. A boundary could even be how close someone comes to you. Another is it's not alright for someone to yell at you or curse at you, though not all boundaries are so obvious. When someone crosses our boundaries, we feel violated. But boundaries aren't effective unless they are well known, and we don't all have the same boundaries. You can't expect another to respect your boundary if they aren't aware of it. Some people who have been able to take advantage of you in the past may initially be uncomfortable when you start enforcing your boundaries, but don't let that deter you from being true to your boundaries. Your boundaries are always unknown to strangers, so keep this in mind.

I was waiting to meet a friend of mine for lunch that I hadn't seen in a long time. As he approached me to say hello, I noticed he was on his cell phone, shaking his head and looking quite frustrated. When he ended his call, he greeted me and his face was worn and he appeared upset. I asked him what had him so down. He responded that his wife was miserable at her current job and that was making her life (and his, of course) a living hell. She had impossible deadlines imposed on her, along with staff cuts that she felt would bring her and the organization down to a new low. Her boss frequently berated her, often in front of her subordinates. She worked long hours, barely able to spend time with her loved ones.

In this situation, Lena's (my friend's wife) role was as an employee and supervisor. She generally enjoyed her job, except for the interactions she had with her boss. She felt like her creativity was being stumped and she was having a difficult time focusing. Lena wanted to provide for her family and set a good example to her loved ones. I reminded him that Lena's position as a designer was creative, and going to work each day was certainly showing their loved ones responsibility. She was achieving some of her goals. But the things she didn't enjoy about her job were affecting her ability to recognize the good things her job provided, including life and freedom. Lena knew her boss' behavior was causing her stress, but she didn't know what she could do about it. While it's true that we can't control anyone but ourselves, we can set clear boundaries and let people know what's acceptable and what isn't.

I encouraged Lena to have a calm discussion with her boss and to let her supervisor know that she had a difficult time performing at her best when she felt berated. Lena also felt that yelling was an unacceptable form of communication. Further, being yelled at in front of her subordinates undermined Lena and definitely had a negative impact on employee morale. By communicating her needs clearly, Lena was setting a boundary and allowing for a healthier dynamic to be created at work, and she started to take more control over her life.

Take a moment to consider your boundaries.

- What are they?
- Do others know what they are?
- Do others take advantage of you and cross your boundaries?
- How do you feel when this happens?

Be clear about your boundaries and enforce them.

Another way you can take more control over your life is by eliminating negativity as much as possible. Negativity will drain all your energy, your creativity, and rob you of motivation. Maybe you work with someone who complains all the time, or perhaps a loved one always seems to look at the glass as half empty and complains all the time about everything – that things just aren't good enough. How do you feel after you've been around these people? Maybe you start to feel tired, or you start to look at your life with a negative spin. When you find yourself in these situations, get out of them as soon as possible if you can. If it's a conversation, gracefully find your way out of the conversation. Let your companions know, "this conversation is making me uncomfortable. Let's discuss something else." You could steer the conversation to a more productive or positive topic without them even knowing. If you have to leave the room, then do. I'm not suggesting you be irresponsible. You likely have a job, a house, bills to pay, a family to support that loves you very much. I'm encouraging you to be responsible for your joy and happiness and your feelings of abundance. You can choose how you perceive your surroundings.

A friend of mine has shared a rather co-dependent relationship with her mother, even though she's a grown woman. Her mother would call to complain about how much she disliked her job, her apartment, and talk about how lonely she was, and how she is worried about everything. One day my friend said to her mother, "Mom, you know that you attract what you focus on, right? The more you focus on how unhappy you are with things, the more you'll experience unhappiness. Why don't you try to focus on the things that are right with your job, your home, and your relationships and stop worrying about things that are not in your control?" Her mother didn't know what to say and she ended the conversation quickly. I reminded my friend that it wasn't her responsibility to make her mother feel better, it was her responsibility to take care of herself. Life is too short to spend it with people who don't add something positive to your life. Now, I'm not saying to run away from your problems or issues, but rather confront them, and if they can't be resolved, consider what all your options are. Again, you are designing your dream life.

So far I've asked you to:

- De-clutter
- Eliminate your energy drains
- Remove yourself from negativity
- Analyze your motivations
- Stop multi-tasking
- Begin journaling
- Track how you spend your time
- Identify the roles in your life

That's a lot of changes! But well worth your time and energy.

If you want to take control of your life, you've got to make your life work for you.

The major relationships you have in your life will be impacted by the changes that you make. But no one will be more affected than you. So with that in mind, where do you fit into a list of important people in your life? Do you often put yourself first, or others first? Are you trying to please your partner? Your children? Your parents? Your boss? Your friends?

I'd like you to do an exercise that will identify the things you do because you have to do them for someone else, and the things you want to do for yourself.

Label the first column: **Things I do for Others**

Label the second column: **Things I want to do for Me**

Things I do for Others	Things I want to do for Me
1. Drive the carpool on Tuesday/Thursday	1. Take a vacation
2. Pick up Kristi's dry-cleaning	2. Sleep late on weekends
3. Have my parents over for dinner every Sunday	3. Have a guys' night out
etc	etc

Be exhaustive and list as many things as you can think of. You undoubtedly do a lot of things for others; try to name them all. Conversely, you probably have a lot of things you'd like to do for yourself, get down as many as you can think of.

Reflecting on your list, which side is longer?

The "Do for Others" list?

or

The "Do for Me" list?

Are there things on the "Do for Me" list that you can start doing now? What about in a week? Will setting clearer boundaries help reduce one side of the list? What about eliminating negativity? Will that take anything off the "To Do" list? What can you do to have more balance between your lists?

This chapter has hopefully allowed you to get to know your own life a little better. For many of us, events and situations and even people sneak up on us over time and before we know it, our lives are nothing like the dreams we had when we were younger.

Once you can recognize the key elements that are working in a negative fashion in your life, whether it is an interfering boss, demanding children, demanding spouses, demanding parents, or your own tendency to procrastinate and generalize, then you can start building a plan on a foundation of gratefulness and appreciation of your own self-worth that will result in your resounding and continuing success.

Most importantly,

<u>don't</u>

<u>let</u>

<u>fear</u>

drive your life!

If you are constantly in fear,

you aren't living!

Fear is something your mind creates

and

Most of the time never comes true.

Chapter Four

Coping with Barriers

You've begun a journey to improve your life and have started to implement changes. It would be completely normal if you found yourself experiencing a range of emotions. At times you may feel overwhelmed, anxious, even scared. You may also feel like you're encountering barriers, or reaching a plateau. So how can you break through the barriers and keep moving in the right direction? It's important that you take care of yourself during this exciting time.

First, I encourage you to honor your progress. Over the past few chapters, you've dealt with examining your perceptions, motivations and relationships in your life. You've completed a series of different exercises designed to help you on your journey. This work isn't always easy. Congratulations for making it this far! This chapter will discuss different methods and ideas to help you support yourself.

As you know, **when you change your mind - you can change your life**. Think of this work as **designing a road map** to reach your favorite destination. The journey will be exciting, exhilarating, and at times you may feel a little anxiety. You're heading into territory that may be new to you. But with any journey, there will be many worthwhile moments that will bring you contentment, and your life will be all the better for taking the trip.

In previous chapters, we've touched on the concept of the negative tape that plays in the back of our minds from time to time. The negative messages keep us from reaching our full potential. You're making a conscious effort to reprogram perceptions and your imagined limitations that were previously set by past experiences. Everything you've learned to this point can be considered tools in your tool kit for improving your life. One of the most effective tools in your arsenal is visualization.

Creative visualization is more than just positive thinking. It's a method used to create harmony and prosperity in your life. We use visualization quite frequently; it's a powerful force in our subconscious minds. For instance, have you ever thought of someone, perhaps a friend you haven't spoken to in a long time, or a family member you've lost touch with, and later, perhaps within days or within moments, your phone rings and guess who is on the line? Or you go to your mailbox and a letter has arrived from this friend? Ever get a surprise in your email box from someone who'd been on your mind? You have created this connection, just by thinking of this person. Now imagine if you use your power of creative visualization with intention? What do you think you'd be able to create? Imagine what you could accomplish.

Henry Ford, the famous pioneer of the automobile industry, once said,

"If you think you can do a thing or think you can't do a thing, you're right." What you believe to be true, what you perceive to be true, will be true for you.

Let's say you believe:
"I only attract men/women who are unsuitable for me."
With this belief system in place, you can bet those are the only kinds of partners who will be attracted to you.

"I will never get that raise."
If you feel this way, you'll probably not even ask for the raise, nor get one.

"I am always broke."
This thought focuses on lack...a lack of wealth.

"I just know the test results are going to be bad."
Sounds like the reaction to the test results are going to be bad.

"He'll never pick me."
With this belief system in place, he may not even notice you.

"I could never look like that."
"I could never be so lucky."
"I'll never make enough money."

You're right!
If you think you won't or you can't, you will be right every time!

Okay, if the above statements could be true,
can't the following also be true?

"I'm attractive and people like me."
"I have a good shot at that promotion."
"I'm going to have that car by the end of the year."
"I'll find the job that's perfect for me."

The answer is YES! It's important to be aware of your thoughts and intentions, because you are subconsciously creating your reality all the time. Creative visualization works best when you are calm, still, and quiet. You should think about something positive in your life that you would like to have or experience.

- Focus on this, and imagine how you will feel when you have achieved this goal.
- Quiet your mind so you are able to focus solely on this thing.
- Create a mental picture of this thing, person, or activity. Really see it in your mind.
- As you picture it, think of it as if it already exists in your life.

- Enjoy the positive feeling you receive from this.
- Stay with your visualization for several minutes.

Throughout the day, think of your visualization often. Continue to imagine it as if it is yours already. Think of it as if you are living it at the moment. The more positive emotions you channel to this thought, the better you will feel, and the more focus you have on your visualization, the more you are creating it, bringing it into reality. Do this daily, and often. If negative thoughts creep in, stop the tape. Replace it with your vision. Visualization is similar to meditation. You can think of it as meditating with intention. Remember that the more positive energy you send out, the more you receive. On the converse, the more negativity you produce, the more negativity you receive.

Use your conscious thoughts to bring the things you want to you.

You live your life in a rhythm. It's important to create a healthy rhythm for your physical body as well as your emotional body. Waking at the same time each morning and going to bed at the same time each night is one way you can set your body on a healthy schedule. We've all heard about the importance of getting enough sleep each night and yet it's the one thing that most us will sacrifice. Maybe we work late, stay up to watch a movie, or hustle to get our chores done while the children are sleeping. Whatever the reason, we rob ourselves of important downtime. I encourage you to set your body on a schedule. Perhaps you only need 6 hours sleep each night to feel like a go-getter in the morning, or maybe you need 10 hours. Whatever your body needs, I urge you to honor it. If we don't nurture our physical being, we'll see the effects in our emotional, mental and spiritual bodies.

If you don't currently get some sort of exercise on a regular basis, I challenge you to begin. It is important to move your body a little bit each day. It improves breathing, circulation, clears your mind...the benefits of exercise are well documented. While this chapter is not about weight loss or enhancing your physical being, everything you learn in this book will work best when you are in good health and taking care of your body.

You don't have to join a gym, and you don't have to run a marathon. You can do jumping jacks or go for a nice peaceful walk around the block, enjoying the surroundings. Once you get going, it's really not so bad. Meet up with a neighbor, a friend and make it a habit. You can help each other keep on schedule. Enjoy the social time with others and your body will feel great at the end of the walk. In the winter, it's more difficult to get outside, so use the stairs in your home, or go to a mall and walk around and around. Sometimes you have to get creative, but if you move around a little every day, your body will perform better for you.

Commit in your calendar or date book, the time you will devote to exercise or moving your body. If you have 15 minutes each day, write it into your schedule. Entering this "me" time into your calendar will help your commitment and you're more likely to do it and stick with it. If you already exercise on a regular basis, write that down in your date book. At the end of the week, reflect on your calendar and give yourself a little gold star or smiley face for every "me" time appointment you honored.

Breathing techniques can be extremely useful for dealing with stressful or uncomfortable situations. When people feel stress, they typically breathe quickly and the breaths are shallow. An effective way to calm yourself in times of stress:

- Slow down. Become aware of your breathing.
- Make your body still.
- Breathe in deeply, and slowly through your nostrils.
- Hold your breath for five seconds and release slowly through your mouth.
- You should feel your diaphragm deflate.
- Repeat several times, slowly.
- Again, be aware of how your body feels when you release. Imagine your anxiety or stress leaving your body as your breath leaves your body.

*If at any time you become dizzy or light headed, stop and let your body return to its normal rhythm. If you have any medical conditions, check with your doctor first.

www.stephenmark.com

Another technique involves laying still on a flat, comfortable surface. Again, become aware of your breathing, and attempt to breathe slowly and deeply. Feel your abdomen as it rises with each inhalation, and as it drops with each exhalation. Envision your breath moving throughout your entire body. Keeping your lips closed, draw in air through your nose. As you take in air, visualize your diaphragm filling with oxygen, filling your lungs. When you exhale, feel your abdomen sinking. As you feel the rise and release of your body, relax your face, your throat, and feel your chest open, all the while releasing tension and stress. Continue to focus on your breathing, taking deep breaths and settle into a fluid rhythm. You should feel relaxed as the stress and anxiety leaves your body. I personally use this method to help control my debilitating migraines on a daily basis.

Since we're so used to doing, doing, doing for others, most of us rarely make time for ourselves. In addition to getting enough rest, we also need time to recharge our batteries, get back to neutral. Rituals are an excellent way to do this. I'm not talking about spells and rituals and magic. I mean a ritual, which is something you do with regularity. Some people consider taking a bath with their favorite songs playing in the background and candles lit, a ritual. While this type of ritual is relaxing, I want you to expand your concept of a ritual. Others consider working out at the gym, dancing to loud music, or sitting outside enjoying nature a ritual. It is time just for you, when you do something that enriches your spirit. Treat your ritual as though it is an important business meeting, and I want you to regularly schedule an appointment with YOU on your calendar each week.

Rituals are one way for you to stay focused on yourself. They are things for you to look forward to. You can receive inspiration, exhilaration, and relaxation by performing regular rituals. Examples of some rituals include:

- Visiting a park, lake, or river. Sit quietly and admire the beauty and peace of nature and sights around you. Listen to all the sounds of nature. Look around and see what you notice that you haven't before.

- Get a massage, facial, manicure, pedicure or reflexology treatment.
- Visit your local library.
- Check out a museum.
- Enroll in a class you find interesting at your local college or community center or consider taking music lessons. Something just for you.
- Have a relaxing cup of tea at a charming bookstore or coffee shop.
- Eat a meal at a restaurant you've never visited. Try something new.
- Check out a botanical garden or new hiking trail.

The possibilities are endless. Regular outings with your friends or a special date night with your partner are also worthy diversions from your hectic schedule and will help you feel rejuvenated. Your rituals don't have to be spent alone, but they should be focused on things that bring you comfort or joy.

In the last chapter I brought up the importance of keeping a journal. A journal is a great ally on this journey of change. I encourage you to not only journal your feelings, fears, anxieties, and anything that comes up for you, but remember to begin each entry with a statement of **gratitude about the abundance in your life.** Use visualization techniques in your journal. As you shift your perceptions, your life will also begin to shift, in a positive direction!

When we have mental/emotional clutter, it's difficult to focus on anything. Have you ever just wanted to unload? Let someone know they hurt your feelings, or that they disappointed you? You're angry and frustrated, and until you dump the garbage, you won't be able to focus on creating the good stuff. When this happens to me, this is when I write what I call "the angriest letter I never sent." That's right. **I don't send the letter,** but you can be sure I write the letter.

It's perfectly healthy to acknowledge and even feel anger. The slippery slope is what you do with your anger. The angry letter is how I deal with this personally. I sit down and start writing freely like we all did when we were kids. I don't check for grammar, punctuation or spelling because it does not matter. This document won't be seen by anyone but me, so it doesn't need to be perfect. It's releasing for me to get the words on paper, and I imagine as the words flow out of me, my anger is flowing out at the same time. I've written letters that were almost eight pages long! There is no right or wrong way to do this; **the only rule is that this letter does not get delivered.** You get back what you put out, so imagine the negativity you'd set yourself to receive if you sent this letter out into the world!

When you are done writing, you can read over your letter if you like. Read it over a couple of times if necessary. After you've read your letter, decide if you are truly finished. When you are done, set the letter aside for a moment. Visualize your anger as a dark funnel cloud, similar to what a tornado would look like. As you visualize this cloud, watch it transform into a thin ribbon. It is now a thin, long ribbon that is tied to the delete key on your computer keyboard. As you hit the delete or escape key, forever erasing your angry letter, visualize your ribbon of anger becoming smaller and smaller, until it disappears and you cannot see it anymore. When you hit the delete button on your computer, you're purging your computer, and your life of the negative emotions that were trapped inside. Dump your garbage as often as you need to so you can keep your life open to creating and experiencing the good stuff. If you hand wrote a letter, shred it so no one else reads it. As you shred it, imagine all that anger and pain being shredded into nothing.

The popularity of blogs has exploded in the last couple of years. Anyone can create a blog, or online journal, about anything. (This is NOT the place to post your "garbage" or angry letter or any other personal information). You may want to create a blog to keep in touch with family and friends, share your experiences, or ask for encouragement. You can also locate a number of online support communities that allow users from all over the world to give each other advice and support.

How do you feel when you're walking down the street and a stranger smiles at you? In our hyper technological world, it seems our personal interactions become more and more limited. We text and we send emails, sometimes we actually make phone calls, but we spend less and less time face-to-face with other human beings. It isn't hard to feel disconnected. That's why I love the "Pay It Forward" concept.

In 2000, actors Kevin Spacey, Helen Hunt, and that kid that everyone loved from the Sixth Sense, Haley Joel Osment, made the concept of Pay It Forward come to life in a blockbuster movie of the same name. (The movie was adapted from the novel by Catherine Ryan Hyde). The concept is basically about **doing random acts of kindness for strangers, for no particular reason at all.** You do something nice for them, and because of what you did for them, this stranger will in turn do something kind for someone else, and on the cycle goes.

I read an article recently about a gentleman who started a chain of good will while passing through a drive-through coffee chain. I'll call the gentleman Peter. The driver in the car behind Peter was honking his horn repeatedly, urging Peter to hurry up. The driver was clearly frustrated. Instead of responding with anger or frustration, what did Peter do?

He paid for the coffee of the impatient man in the car behind him. And do you know how Mr. Impatient-Honking-Horn responded? Humbled by Peter's actions, he in turn paid for the coffee of the customer behind him. Peter began a chain of good will that lasted for over two hours! The manager at the coffee chain was reported as saying, "We've never seen anything like it. It went on for a couple of hours. My employees were incredibly touched. Most of us don't get to see the Pay It Forward idea in action. This was really something."

How good would you feel if you were Peter? Imagine you started a two-hour chain of good will! It's difficult to feel down when you're

　　　　　　　　　　　　　　　　www.stephenmark.com

doing charitable things for others, and it can be something as simple as a smile, saying hello, or picking up the tab for coffee, putting money in a parking meter, or helping someone find their car in a crowded parking lot.

Doing for others energizes us and makes us feel more connected.

I challenge you to Pay It Forward at least once each week for a month. After each experience, journal what you did and how it made you feel. Random acts of kindness can certainly be anonymous. Remember, you're not doing it for the recognition, but at the same time, don't be shy. Tell your friends what you're doing and encourage them to do the same. Think about how many generous acts can be born from just one act in the span of one month. You could increase the goodwill in your community exponentially.

Another way to feel connected to others is to volunteer some time. It may be as little as an hour a month or even an hour a week. Maybe one of your rituals can involve volunteering at an organization that needs some help. Virtually all non-profit organizations need help. There is no shortage of the types of organizations that rely on volunteerism: animal shelters, family violence centers, mentoring organizations, hospice, and many more. Contact your local chambers of commerce or your local newspaper for a complete listing of non-profit organizations in your community who are in need. It's another way that you can generate goodwill in your community and feel gratitude.

Let's talk about when those nagging thoughts creep into your head, and you begin to doubt yourself or your progress, or even your abilities. We've discussed the power of creative visualization, and I will continue to encourage you to use this tool daily. Sometimes it is difficult to **let go of our fear or anxiety**, so I like to use a technique I call the "What If" game.

First, I identify what I'm afraid of or troubled by. It is often useful to make a list. I make three columns so it looks as below:

Issue	I feel	What if I'm right
Job search	Nervous, scared	I will be broke
	Which leads to…	
Being broke	Scared	I can't pay my bills
	Which leads to…	
Behind to creditors	Scared	Wreck my credit
	Which leads to…	
Bad credit	Apprehensive	So I have bad credit

I begin by starting with the main issue that's troubling me. I identify how it makes me feel. And then I go to the next step and play a little of the worst-case scenario game.

So what if I'm right?

So what if I'm broke?

So what if I can't pay my creditors?

Then what?

When I work through these issues, it becomes clear that I'm nervous that my credit will be damaged. In the grand scheme of my life, I can live with damaged credit. When I reduce my stress level about my job search, I release the fear, and I can begin to focus again. And what do I do with that focus? I start my creative visualization. Now I'm no longer anxious, and I'm focused on creating what I want.

When we focus on what we lack, we produce more lack. In the "What If" scenario, you acknowledge the negative possibilities you are fearful of becoming reality. You acknowledge, but don't focus on them. Release them, and release the anxiety. Focus on the success by following up with "What If" Part 2 – shown below. Here's what the same issues look like with the positive possibilities plugged in:

Issue	I feel	What if I'm right
Job search	Excited, hopeful	I get the job I want
	Which leads to…	
Financial freedom	Excited	Easily pay my bills
	Which leads to…	
Begin saving	Secure	Start saving money
	Which leads to…	
Vacation	Excited, happy	I get to celebrate, relax

Wow!

"What If" Part 2 looks much better, doesn't it? I worked through my fear, shifted my perceptions, and now I'm focusing on financial freedom and a vacation! Be conscious of what you focus on. First clear the fear. Then focus on the positive.

Someone I know is an anxious worrier. He raised two great kids and welcomed his grandchildren into his life. Lately he's been getting tired. In his mid-fifties, he has no savings and works jobs to pay his bills.

Often he will call one of his children in a panic. "There's no work this week! How am I going to pay the rent?" When they get the call, they remind him that focusing on his lack of money will create a lack of money.

Recently, he received a phone call from a bill collector for an old debt he was sure he had previously paid off. After the phone call with the pushy collections representative, he was completely convinced this company was going to take him to court and sue him; he was also convinced he didn't owe the money. I asked him if he'd run through the worst-case scenario.

He figured out that the worst-case scenario was that this bill collection company might sue him in small claims court. The worst outcome could be that a magistrate court would in fact hold him responsible for the debt, and he'd have to make monthly payments to the creditor. "But that's just it, I don't have the money to pay them," he cried. I reminded him that if, in fact, he decided he was absolutely going to court with this company, that's where he'd likely end up. If he decided he was absolutely going to lose the case, then he probably would. And if the worst thing came to pass, he would be forced to pay this creditor $5 per month, possibly up until his death. In the grand scheme of his life, $5 per month hardly seemed like it was worth the stress it was causing him. It never occurred to him that his life was too precious to spend countless hours worrying about things, when, if in fact his worst-case scenario came to pass, he really could live with the outcome after all.

When you have an important decision to consider, try using the worst-case scenario. Ask yourself:

- **What is the absolute worst thing that could happen?**

- **How will it impact me?**

- **How will I deal with a negative outcome?**

- **Can I live with it?**

                    www.stephenmark.com

I also encourage you to determine if it's worth your time to be anxious and stressed over things that are not life-threatening. Things happen outside of our control, but we can always control our reaction. As with the "What If" game, take the same situation and run it through the best-case scenario. Ask yourself:

- **What is the best possible outcome?**

- **How will I feel?**

- **Who else will be impacted by this outcome?**

- **How will we celebrate?**

Always take the issues in front of you and run them through two scenarios; what would be the worst case and what will be the best case? Then make a conscious decision to focus on the best possible outcome.

It's important to have a strong support system in place. Your support system might include your spouse, partner, co-workers, friends, family members, whomever you trust and feel comfortable sharing your aspirations and disappointments with. When you share your goals with others, remember that it does two things: it affirms your commitment and allows others to encourage you. Some people find support in online communities, as previously discussed. Wherever you find your support, be sure to ask for help when you need it.

Meditation is another tool that can prove useful in your self-improvement journey. It helps the mind and body to be still, and helps quiet anxiety. There are several ways and places you can meditate. I meditate for 15 minutes before going to bed each night. A friend of mine does it before she gets out of bed in the morning. You can meditate whenever you have a few minutes for yourself.

There is no right or wrong way to meditate. The space you choose however is important, because you need to be in a tranquil surrounding, one that is pleasing to you. Some people will burn incense or light candles, generally to create an environment of serenity. You can use a CD and do guided meditations, which is where a soothing voice on the CD will help you to slow your breathing, clear your mind, and usually provide an image for you to visualize in your mind. Sometimes they suggest a chant or a phrase for you to focus on. Your subconscious mind is incredibly powerful and the thoughts you focus on during meditation become powerful as well.

To meditate you simply need your body and your mind to be still. When thoughts aren't racing through your head, you make it easier to access your subconscious, which is your ally in both creation and solving the issues that trouble you. There are limitless resources available online and at bookstores, where the shelves are overflowing with information and methods on meditation. There are also many communities that have spiritual centers where group meditations are offered.

A good friend of mine has been meditating every evening for more than 3 years now. She has found that she sleeps more soundly, and often wakes up feeling like she has found the solutions to some of her problems. "I focus on a question I need answered at the end of my meditation. When I get up in the morning, I've worked it through. Actually, my subconscious worked on it while I slept." This is a technique I encourage you to try, because when you put your subconscious mind to work on something, you have a helper. You don't have to do all the work, in fact you can get a good night's rest and let someone else take over!

Organizations have mission statements, do you? That's right, a mission statement. In the last chapter we talked about the importance of having boundaries, but a mission statement is like a personal motto or mantra. When you have a mission statement, you have clarity about your purpose and focus.

Think about what your mission statement could be…

    www.stephenmark.com

- Your mission statement should be five sentences or less. Brief! Simple!

- It should illustrate **what you want to focus on.**

- Keep it positive. No negative language (ie "don't, won't, can't")

- Include traits, behaviors and values that you hold important.

- This statement should guide you each day.

- How will your mission statement affect different areas of your life.

Your mission statement is not concrete, it can be ever-changing and you can modify it, as you need to. It should act as an anchor for you, a resource and a guide to keep you focused. Below is an example to help you get started. You could also check out the mission statement of a company you do business with and use that as a guide.

I will/want/choose to _____

so that _____. I will accomplish this by doing/being/learning _____.

In case I haven't made the point yet, attitude is important!

I know of and have read about people that wake before 4:00am each day, to get up and stand outside in sometimes freezing, usually wet weather, lifting huge bundles weighing more than a small man, lugging around heavy packages all day, standing during most of their 12 hour work shift. And these same guys, you'd be hard pressed to meet a happier bunch.

Meet the fishmongers at the world famous Pike Place Fish Market, located in Seattle, Washington. The market is one of the most well-known landmarks of the Emerald City, behind the Space Needle of course. So how do these people do it?

They operate by four guiding principles:

- **Choose Your Attitude.** Each person on the team makes a conscious effort when they wake up in the morning, about what kind of attitude they will have for that day. As one fishmonger said, "I can't control anyone but me. If I begin my day consciously choosing to have a good attitude and to make a difference to at least one other person, I'm deciding to have a good day."

- **Play.** They find a way to have fun, doing their jobs. They know that happiness and fun are contagious.

- **Make Their Day.** The fishmongers are having fun, and they want to share that with others. They do their best to include outsiders in their good time. They understand that one positive interaction with another person might just make that person's day.

- **Be Present.** The staff at the market makes every customer the most important customer. They don't try to do a bunch of things at once (remember the idea about doing ONE thing at a time?), they remain fully present so the exchange they have with other people is always authentic and personable.

What can we learn from some people that fling fish around the marketplace? The lesson here is that no matter what you do, who you are, where you are from, you can change your life when you have a positive attitude.

Attitude does matter in everything you do!

So remember to dump the garbage when you feel overloaded. Run through the "What If" scenario when you're worried or anxious. Visualize the life you want, meditate and journal about it. Do random acts of kindness and seek out support when you need it. Your toolbox is full of resources you will need to be successful!

Part Two

Ok,
I Want To Be Successful,
But I Don't Know What I Want

Chapter Five

What Should I Be Doing?

Oscar Wilde once said, "To live is the rarest thing in the world. Most people exist, that is all."

So how are you living? Do you have the career you want for yourself? What about your home, are you living in a place that brings you pride or inner peace? Could the relationships in your life use a tune up? If you're reading this book, you've come to the realization that you don't have everything you want…yet.

In Chapter 3, you identified the different roles you play in your life and the role others have in yours. Research shows that pop culture, news and our families provide the strongest influences for developing the values and interests we hold as adults. How do your relationships and values affect the choices you make in your life? Do you compromise to make others happy? How will making changes for you affect those around you?

If you divided your life into the following areas:

Home
Family
Personal/Romantic relationships
Career/Job

and then rated your satisfaction with each, what would that look like? Are you satisfied with where you live? Do you have meaningful relationships in your life that offer you joy and comfort? Is your relationship with your children fulfilling? What about your relations with your siblings or parents? On a scale of 1 – 10, score your current level of satisfaction. After some reflection, next to each area you've scored, make an asterisk next to the areas you want to improve this year. Is there one area in particular that stands out? What areas on your list scored highest? Where do you think you should devote the most energy?

Let's start by focusing on your present career. Do you wake up every morning excited about facing the challenges of the day? Or is it a challenge to get up to face the day?

Take a moment to reflect on your current job. Answer the following questions:

1. *What excites me about my job?*

2. *What are the benefits afforded to me by working here?*

3. *What percentage of the time do I feel inspired? Challenged?*

4. *Is this job tuned into my talents and passions?*

5. *My   key   motivation   for   working   here   is:*
   _____

Don't be surprised if your motivation is financial. Most people work because they have to - it's not a matter of choice. Living in society means we have to pay for things: houses, student loans, car loans, utilities, food, day care and the clothes we wear.

You could be motivated by money, prestige, opportunity or obligation. Whatever the reason you are in your current position, if it's not where you want to be, consider where you do want to be.

It's time to create a new job for yourself if:

- You experience the Sunday blues ~ that dread that creeps into your body about half way through Sunday, dreading Monday morning.
- You're consistently late to work for reasons in your control.
- By mid-year you've used all your vacation and sick days.
- You avoid interactions with your colleagues and/or boss.
- You spend time complaining about your co-workers or to your co-workers on a regular basis at work and home using your energy and the energy from those that surround you.
- Your only motivation for going to the office is to receive a paycheck.
- You frequently procrastinate and are operating without a professional goal.

My friend, we'll call Jeff, used to work in a job that offered him no satisfaction. Sure, the salary was decent and Jeff was able to pay his rent and his car note, but he dreaded not only the eight hours in the office, but the 45 minute or longer commute and spent many days waiting out the clock so he could race to his car and head home at the end of the day. Does this sound familiar? He said, "It was like a marathon and I just had to make it to the finish line at the end of the day. I didn't like the work, my co-workers were crazy, and nobody there seemed to know what they were doing. No one was focused and the atmosphere was chaotic. People were all running in different directions and not getting anywhere. It was the longest year of my life!"

Why would Jeff take a job that made him miserable? Pressure. **Fear.** Jeff had been laid off from a job that had offered him great personal and professional satisfaction. After two months on the job market, he was fearful about getting further into debt, so he took the first job he was offered, at the Crazy People Place, as it came to be known. The worst stressor for him was that he wasn't productive or creative anymore, drained of all his energy from all the fear and pressure. "It was impossible for me to achieve anything, there was just too much turmoil and negativity everywhere. I really felt like I wasn't producing anything and that's not like me. I'm a team player and I enjoy challenging work. I just don't want to be challenged to go to work."

Unable to focus, Jeff also felt unable to even look for another job. "I felt too disorganized. I couldn't get my head into anything. And in that environment I certainly didn't feel like I had anything to offer another employer. I felt totally stuck and miserable." Jeff didn't believe he had anything to offer, so he didn't even look for another position elsewhere.

> **Remember that what you believe to be true becomes true for you.**

To Jeff's relief, the Crazy People Place ran their operating account too low, and his position was eliminated in an effort to save money. "It was such a weight off my shoulders. I thought I'd be afraid, suddenly no job, no income, but you know what's weird? I didn't experience any fear at all, only a sense of relief. Like wow, I survived that, and now I can collect myself and focus on getting what I want. I resolved to get clear on what I needed in an employer, and seek out the perfect job for me. I did not focus on my finances, I focused on what I wanted and needed professionally."

A year later, Jeff works for himself. When he was able to escape the chaotic environment of his previous job, it allowed him to get reacquainted with his own passions and talents. He revisited his passion for helping others, and he went on to start a firm that offers business training seminars. Today he boasts a heavy workload, full client list, and a healthy bank account. Jeff let go of the fear that was quite literally blocking his ability to create the career he wanted. When he did so, he began reaping the benefits.

Remember the "What If" technique? Why not apply it to your current career? Ask yourself "this is what I'm doing now, but what if…?" Allow yourself to daydream for a moment. What would your dream job look like? Where would it be? What would you be doing? What kinds of people would you be working with?

Everyone is good at something; usually we're talented at many things. What happens when our talents match our passions? For example, I'm talented when it comes to helping others. But am I passionate about it? Absolutely! Would I want to utilize that talent in a professional capacity? A resounding YES! People who enjoy their careers have generally found a way to match their talents with their passions.

If you have trouble defining your special talent, ask your friends or family. Some questions to ask yourself and them:

- *What do you see as my biggest strength?*

- *What area do you think I could improve?*

- *What is one of my unique talents?*

- *If I was featured in the newspaper, what would the story be about?*

Once you identify your talents, begin to honor your gifts. You probably take your skills for granted as we all tend to do. I want you to start to be it, believe it, share it with others!

Remember that you need to practice your gifts and talents. If you're not currently using your gifts, think of ways you can. Can you share them by volunteering or mentoring? Is there a class or workshop you could participate in? You will master your skills by utilizing them. If you start to do what you love in your life, you can do it in your career as well. Remember, just like anything else in life, you can learn to master your talents and passions.

This planet is made up of a lot of energy – you can choose to go with the flow, or against it. If your current job, professional or personal status is making you weary, disappointed or disenchanted, you're going against the flow of your life. If things are extremely difficult, they aren't the right things for you. This applies to relationships, jobs, hobbies, whatever it is that isn't easy for you. Now I don't mean to say that there really is truly an "easy" button (as advertised on television), and you have to find it and then…poof! Life gets easy. What I am saying is that when you really pay attention to your feelings and intuition, you can tell when you're going against the flow of your life.

When our validation comes from outside sources, places other than us, we do things and choose experiences designed to please others not ourselves. **We have to be present in our own lives.** You are responsible for pleasing yourself and attracting situations and people into your life that will compliment your wants and desires. Yes, it's that darn power of attraction thing again; it's always at work!

What can you do when you are in a job or career that isn't meeting your needs? The quick answer is simple - if you don't like it, then don't do it, if you don't have to or find a way to make it more enjoyable. Spend time doing the things you do enjoy and you'll attract more things you enjoy. Work on a special project that brings you joy. If there is a corporate project you'd like to be part of, volunteer to help. Plant a garden, build a fence, paint a picture, cook a special seven course meal, start a community or civic group in your neighborhood, do fundraising for a cause that you hold dear, write a novel, run a marathon…tap into your desire and just do it. You will find inspiration by doing things you enjoy. In your inspired state, you'll be more ready to build your life around things and people you enjoy. Ever notice how "successful" people seem to attract people and opportunities easily?

You could look at the successful people in your life with envy, or you could follow their lead and copy what they do while keeping your individualism and passions alive. Again, do something you really enjoy and you open up your life to create more enjoyment.

Zero in on what it is you do want in your new career, the one you're going to create for yourself. You're already clear on what you don't want, but your task here is to focus on the "wants" instead of "don't wants." Get specific, for example:

- **I want to work from home one day each week**
- **I want to live near the ocean**
- **I want to make a salary of $ XXXXX**

- **I want to lead x people**
- **I want to have an office with a window**
- **I want my hours in the office to be 10am to 6pm**
- **I want to live in the Mountains**

That's right: get very specific. Now visualize this job. See yourself walking into your new office, watch yourself utilizing your talents and feeling your passion for the work. Pretend you already have this job. Notice how it makes you feel. Make time throughout the day to visualize your new job, remembering that visualization is the most powerful method for creation.

Now that you are focusing on what you want to be doing, create an action plan. Your action plan should include details and deadlines for what you are going to do, and when you are going to do it.

Otherwise it's just a list, and not an action plan.

For example:

Action	Completion date
Update resume	Thursday
Contact references I plan to use	Friday
Search classifieds	Today and every day
Search online job banks	Each evening, starting tonight*
Prepare cover letters	Friday

*Never, ever spend your time at your present job looking for new jobs. It is not only unfair to your present employer, but the odds are good that it will not go unnoticed, which could lead to difficult situations.

What can you do if you're unsure what career you'd like to pursue? Visit a career counselor or get a life coach, who will often ask you a series of questions to determine where your interests and skill sets fall. Read over the classifieds to get acquainted with the jobs that are available, search the internet. Go to your local library and research trade and business journals. And don't forget to ask your librarian who is a wealth of information! You can also take career assessment tests online, many times at no charge at all. Research salary calculators to determine what positions in your desired field of employment pay. Do your homework!

You are an extraordinary employee and individual, so how do you let prospective employers know? You'll want a dynamic resume. Visit online resume banks to view some popular formats and buzzwords. Employers receiving hundreds of applications for a limited number of job openings have only your cover letter and resume to determine if you are a potential fit for their company. If you need assistance with your resume, look online for companies that will prepare your resume and cover letters at nominal rates.

To stand out in the crowd, you need to build your brand. You're marketing an amazing asset – you! When you build a brand you are letting people know what they can expect. Think about Nike, the popular sports brand. What do you think of when you hear the brand name? Yes, their trademark swoosh comes to mind, but you might also think:

- Popular

- Quality

- Expensive/inexpensive

- Easy to find

- Sneakers, t-shirts, sporting gear

The brand calls to mind all the things Nike is. What about REI? Do you picture outdoor adventure gear? The brand symbolizes getting out and enjoying the great outdoors. What would your brand conjure? Dependable, creative, motivated, productive?

What makes you stand out and makes you different from the competition? You need to market your uniqueness. What's your attitude? What vibe do you put out there?

Talk to your friends or colleagues who are working in fields that interest you. Ask questions and find out what the current business trends and challenges are. Attend business luncheons and seminars; local chambers of commerce usually host these monthly. Meet other professionals and expand your network. Networking is an excellent way to expand your career search. You'll meet people who are in the know, and you'll find out about upcoming opportunities for advancements, trainings or jobs that may not even get posted.

In a previous chapter I mentioned the idea of getting rid of the annoyances in your life, the things that clutter it up, add chaos. You can't have room in your life for new stuff if your life is filled to the brim with old or useless stuff. Clear your space of clutter. If you have stockpiled months of memos on the corner of your desktop, or have 1000 sticky notes plastered all over your office, get to work! Organize your reports or important papers so they are easily accessed from a filing cabinet, sorted by priority. Turn the sticky notes into one list that you affix to your bulletin board so the tasks can be seen easily. Recycle old papers, junk mail and old magazines. Create order in your working space so you are more able to focus.

And don't forget the clutter at home. Out with the old, make room for the new. Especially in your closet! If you have old clothes hanging around that you don't need or wear anymore, donate them to a charity. Make room in your closet for the new clothes that you buy and have for your new job.

In the last chapter we discussed having a personal mission statement. Simply put, those who have a purpose or a goal are more successful than people who don't. It's like I mentioned before, a plan without action, it's just a list.

With a sense of purpose you'll attract others to you with a similar purpose. What is it that you want to accomplish or learn? Write down your purpose. Some examples to help you get started are:

My purpose is to be a catalyst for growth and change.

My purpose is to help others rise and live an extraordinary life.

My purpose is to raise a healthy, loving family.

My purpose is to be a mentor to young people in my community.

My purpose is to create peace in my environment.

Whatever your purpose, write it down and keep it where you can see it. This is a guiding principle, or a theme for your life. Maybe the theme is what you'll work on for the next year; perhaps its something that you'll work on for much longer. It doesn't have to be prolific, like curing cancer or ending world hunger. Your theme can change often. It can be as simple as, "My theme for this year is to laugh often and make others smile." Maybe you change your theme every month. The importance behind it is that it helps you to stay focused on achieving what you want, while moving forward.

Remember the list you worked on at the beginning of this chapter? You rated your satisfaction with different areas of your life. Most people will find that the areas of family and personal relationships can use improvement. Gandhi once said, "The weak can never forgive. Forgiveness is an attribute of the strong." I'd like to explore the concept of forgiveness and how you can use it to your advantage.

Holding on to hurts, pains or keeping grudges is a huge drain to your energy. If you want to feel immediate relief, call someone who hurt or disappointed you in some way, and apologize to them. That's right, YOU apologize to them. If you don't want to call them, just admit to yourself that you forgive them. Tell yourself that you forgive them. It's not about who is right and who is wrong, it's about eliminating barriers to attracting what you want in your life. I promise you that when you let go of the anger, you will feel a renewed sense of energy. You will also be able to replace what was once a negative space with something positive. Don't get weighed down in past mistakes or past hurts. The past is behind you and you'll feel better when you forgive others and forgive yourself. Forgiveness also allows you to achieve more satisfaction in your personal relationships.

Life doesn't just happen to us - we are creating our lives all the time. The goal is to create with intention. It's not just the words and thoughts you use, it's also your intention. If your intention is to have more loving and healthy relationships, **you start by being more loving and healthy**. Remember: Give and you shall receive.

Perhaps you have resentments because you feel like you've made sacrifices for someone in your life. We feel the pressures of family and what's expected of us. For some reason, human beings have the idea that people who love us should inherently know what we need or what we want, without us having to ask for it. As if the entire world are mind readers? How much time and energy, and hurt feelings, could we spare ourselves if we simply asked for what we wanted?

When you become aware of what your needs are, you can start asking for your needs to be met. For example, a retail clerk who has an excellent sales record and is a top performer. His paycheck reflects his stellar sales performance, but he doesn't get feedback from his managers, and becomes unhappy with his job. Obviously, our sales clerk has a need to be appreciated by his supervisors, not by a handsome payday. Our salesperson needs to let his bosses know how he wants to be appreciated. Most people, when asked, will be happy to give you what you need.

Tina had been dating her boyfriend Ron for over a year. They had similar interests and enjoyed each other's company very much. They regularly went on romantic dinner dates and shared holidays with each other's families. Overall they were well suited, but Tina wasn't sure she was happy in the relationship. "Ron is a great guy," she told me. "And I know he loves me because of all the kind things he does for me, and he treats me very well. But he hardly ever says 'I love you.'" What a problem to have! A wonderful, thoughtful, loving partner who treats you well. So I asked Tina what she wanted from Ron. "I guess I need to hear him tell me that he loves me. And not just on special occasions."

I encouraged Tina to let Ron know exactly what she wanted from him. If she wanted Ron to tell her every day that he loves her, that was what she needed to tell him. So one evening, at dinner, Tina shared with Ron that while she was sure she loved him, she needed something more from him. She wanted for him to tell her, regularly.

And do you know what happened? Ron happily obliged. He did love Tina, but he was unaware that she needed to hear it often. Tina asked for what she wanted and she got it. Because she asked for what she wanted and needed. Some people need hugs, others need kisses, some need nothing more than companionship.

Think about what you want from others? What do you expect from:

- Your boss
- Your romantic partner
- Your children
- Your landlord
- Your siblings or parents

Try making a list of the things you want, and who you want it from. Maybe your needs include:

- Appreciation
- Recognition
- Respect
- Affection

This next exercise is another way of setting boundaries, but it's also a tool you can use to get clear on what you want from the major relationships in your life.

You may be in relationships that are unhealthy for you. It's a good idea to take inventory of those you allow in your personal life and decide if they have a positive impact on you. Are you in a relationship with anyone who drains your energy? Remember that energy drains *in essence,* blocks your ability to receive what you want.

I'm not suggesting you get a divorce, break up with your significant other or cut off your relations with family members. Certainly if you have any issues, you may wish to explore dialogue with a licensed mental health professional or licensed counselor. The purpose of examining these relationships is only to encourage you to ask for what you need.

If you are unhappy with your current career, focus on what your positive qualities, talents and abilities are. Reflect on your passions. Use creative visualization to create the job that's perfect for you! Set an action plan and get to work. Build your own unique brand. De-clutter your environments and get rid of the old in order to make room for the new. Choose your theme for this year and keep it posted for you to see. Take responsibility for the relationships in your life. Forgive when necessary. And always ask for what you want. The law of attraction is always at work!

 www.stephenmark.com

Chapter Six

How Do I Know What I Want?

Pretend for a moment that your life up to now, including your partner, career, house, your past and present are mapped out on an enormous blackboard. The drawing includes the greatest moments you've achieved, and your saddest disappointments. It's all there, captured in black and white. Now imagine, you have a magic eraser. You get to erase the parts you aren't satisfied with. Here's an opportunity to re-map and change things around. You can write in new things, erase the old. What a great idea! Take a moment and visualize your blackboard in your mind. What are you going to change?

This is what creating your dream life and change is like. You have the tools in your tool kit to re-map things in your life, and create all new things. I'll say it again, change your mind and you change your life. You choose to live life the way you do.

Now, imagine the blackboard is completely blank. Everything you once knew about yourself has been erased. You get to start all over again. Think about the life you want to map and get your chalk ready. It's time to begin creating your dream life.

As children, most of us believed anything was possible. If our families celebrated Christmas, we believed that Father Christmas (Santa Claus or Kris Kringle) delivered presents to all the children of the world, in a single night, riding in a flying sleigh, led by a band of highly trained reindeer with a leader that has a shiny red nose. We also believed that a little fairy crept into our rooms at night, and offered us gifts for our lost teeth. Perhaps you remember the bouncing, rascally rabbit that took our brightly colored eggs and hid them throughout our yards, and left us jellybeans and chocolates in return for his mischievous behavior. We also believed that it was possible to grow up and turn into a super hero. Boy did we have some imaginations!

As we mature, we begin to doubt that most things are possible. Our sense of wonder and awe gives way to reality, and self-doubt. We watch television and read magazines and learn that women are supposed to be skinny, blonde, and possibly surgically altered. Real men don't cry and they drive expensive sports cars and drink imported beers.

As children we have self-confidence and self-esteem. We believe in our own abilities. **By the time we reach adolescence our perceptions of the world and ourselves shift.** We figure out that we should never stink and start using (deodorant, perfume and aftershave), our hair shouldn't be freeform, but rather perfectly formed (hairspray, hair gel), and a woman should never show her true roots (hair dye). We can only lead fulfilling lives if we own the biggest, the most expensive, and the best. We lose our faith in Father Christmas and believe the world should be full of supermodels. Yikes! What kind of world is this becoming?

As you stand in front of your blank blackboard, you are the architect for your life. Where will you begin? This is an exciting, yet daunting task. How have your past experiences colored your processes? What belief systems do you hold that inhibits you from creating your perfect life?

When my best friend told me in college that he longed to be a police officer, I thought there would be no way that he would do this. It sounded so far-fetched and difficult to do. He'd wanted to do this since he was in high school. He had a life plan he chose at a young age. I saw him as my best friend, a local butcher at the time. I set limits that I should not have. My belief system apparently was tainted.

Are we all this lucky to know what we personally want to do? No, most of us go through life trying to find our passion and what it is that we enjoy doing. He didn't give up on dreaming, he just aligned his dream to coincide with what mattered most to him – in his case, serving the public. Do adults realign their dreams, or do they just give up on dreaming? **Before you thought you couldn't, what did you think you could become?**

When I run into an acquaintance on the street or at my local grocery store, during our quick exchange I am usually asked, "How are you?" I never answer with the following adjectives: fine, good, well, okay. Because I don't want my life to be just good, just fine, just well, or just okay. My response is usually an enthusiastic "Amazing! Or Outstanding!" which tends to get a raised eyebrow and a resulting conversation and "life interaction" in return. I don't waiver; I just smile. I am creating an amazing life, and I'm proud of it. I consciously choose my words to reflect the life I'm living. Often we don't pay attention to our responses and they become automatic. Do you want a "just okay" life? I don't think so. If that were true, you wouldn't be reading this book and filling your toolbox with resources meant to inspire and motivate you.

Best-selling author Gail Sheehy once said, "If we don't change, we don't grow. If we don't grow, we aren't really living." Change is a process and you will slowly begin to adjust your behaviors until they become habits. I challenge you to start talking about your life as you want it to be, using colorful and exciting language to describe yourself, your partner, your home, your career, your family. The old adage about "faking it, until you make it" is at play here. With enough practice, you won't be faking it - you will be living it.

It's time to design your ideal life. Where to begin? You will have to expand your thinking and believe that bigger and better is possible. **Let go of your perceived limitations.** Remember while doing this exercise that anything you want is possible.

Answer these questions:

- **What will your home look like?**

- **Where will you live?**

- **Who will you spend time with?**

- **What kind of things will you do for enjoyment and fun?**

- **What kind of work will you do?**

- **Describe what a normal day for you is like…**

Write your answers down in detail. Sketch, draw or paint it. Visualize the different parts of your life.

Once you've got some ideas, it's time to create what I call a "Dream Board." This project requires a little time and a few materials. You can draw pictures or find images in magazines or online. You'll be looking for images that represent your wishes. For instance, if in your ideal life you spend time relaxing on the shores of Mexico or the Caribbean, find pictures or images depicting beach scenes. Clip out the image and paste it to a poster board or piece of construction paper. Underneath the scene write a caption, explaining what the image represents. For example, "Here I am enjoying the warm and inviting waters during our annual vacation to Mexico."

Your "Dream Board" will end up looking like a collage, with captions. This is also a good place to include your personal mission statement. The idea is to use bold images to visually represent the aspects of your ideal life. Take your time with this project. Find images that really speak to you, and that you find aesthetically pleasing. When you've completed your "Dream Board", give it a prominent position in your home or office. The placement is important because your assignment is to gaze at your "Dream Board" several times each day, look at each image and read the caption to yourself. Don't just skim over the images and captions, reflect on them and begin attracting them into your life.

The "Dream Board" is another method of creative visualization. It's a tool to help you begin to see your life as it truly is, full of possibilities. Take pride in your completed "Dream Board". Think of the satisfaction a young child feels when his or her parents put their artwork up on the refrigerator. They beam with pride every time they enter the kitchen and see their masterpiece in a prominent place for everyone to enjoy. Your "Dream Board" is like the picture on the refrigerator. Be proud and look at it often. Can you remember this wonderful feeling?

You've probably heard the old saying, "a body in motion, stays in motion." The same is true of making changes in your life. Once you begin with small changes, any change, it leads to more change. Don't get overwhelmed at the idea that you have to change everything at once. Once you begin to make even tiny changes, the changes keep coming. So change something. Change anything. Change your hairstyle, rearrange your furniture or drive a different route on your way home. Change makes room for more change.

Several things can prevent us from making changes, and fear generally tops the list. If fear is limiting you, I recommend that you take a deeper look at what it is you are afraid of. Some fears are grounded in cultural or religious beliefs. Others are created through the media. I am not anti-media, but it has to be said that the news media is largely responsible for creating a culture of fear. The negative stories that get reported every morning and evening have us afraid to speak to strangers (you might get mugged!), afraid of people of different ethnicities and cultures (they could be terrorists!), afraid of animals (dogs bite people!) and on and on. Is your fear based on experiences or on your perceptions?

One way to deal with fear is to take more risks. You don't have to skydive or put yourself in physical danger to be a risk taker. You could ask your boss for a raise, you could volunteer to handle a public speaking engagement, you could make a phone call to someone you've been avoiding, you could talk to a total stranger or go to dinner by yourself at a popular restaurant. Stretch outside your comfort zone just a bit and feel the exhilaration and satisfaction. Taking little risks will open you up to experiencing change in your life and help to tone down your fear factor.

Commit to trying <u>at least</u> 3 things in the next month that are outside of your comfort zone.

Write down what it is you'll do and include the date. Afterwards write down how the experience made you feel. Would you do it again? What was the scariest part? What did you discover about yourself by doing it? Would you do it again? Review the following examples:

Task	Date	How it Felt
Go to a popular movie, alone	*Jan 23rd*	*A little scary at first, like everyone was looking at me. But as the movie started, I relaxed and enjoyed myself.*
Talk to a stranger	*Feb 21th*	*I spoke to a woman in the produce section of the market. It was awkward at first, but not as hard as I thought. I am going to practice doing this every time I go to the market.*
Speak at the Rotary Club	*May 5nd*	*I was nervous at first but the audience was attentive and it boosted my confidence.*

  www.stephenmark.com

Often we figure out what we want based on what we know we do NOT want. This is a tricky thing. When you focus on what you know for certain you do not want, you attract what you focus on and along comes more of what makes you unhappy. A tool I have found particularly helpful is to write about it in my journal, but I get creative. Let's say that I go on a blind date and I spend an evening with the most obnoxious woman I've ever met. Whoa! I know she's not the kind of woman I want to spend my time with. I think of the opposite of the qualities Ms. Wrong exhibited, because those are the qualities I want in a soul-mate. My journal entry might look like this:

"I am so grateful for the abundance of loving relationships in my life. I am excitedly awaiting the amazing romantic relationship that I know is on its way, with a partner who is sensitive, caring, compassionate, educated, and funny."

(Ms. Wrong would not be described as having any of the above-mentioned qualities.) If I described the potential mate I had just been on a date with, I'd run the risk of attracting a mate who was arrogant, unfeeling, chauvinistic, and a negative person as a whole. No thanks, I'll work on attracting the amazing one.

The same principle should be applied to all areas of your life. Rather than complain about the job you have, use vivid and rich language to describe the job of your dreams. Speak about the home you want to live in with language that is alive and exciting; don't run down the home you have now. Negativity makes us feel powerless, it robs our creativity, and it spreads. Be thankful for what you have today.

Remember the Pay It Forward concept? Well I have another challenge, just as easy. Increase your awareness of the language you use on a daily basis. The way you talk to others. The way you describe things in your life or other people, be very aware of your words any time you use verbal communication to convey a message. If you find yourself using language that is negative or derogatory, I challenge you to stop. Right then. Catch yourself in the act, and then correct the behavior. The behavior will become a habit if you practice it.

I became aware of the language I was using and altered my verbal communication recently and continue to do so. And that is what I'm asking you to do. When you eliminate the negative talk, you will enjoy your own limelight. People will find you more pleasant to be around and you will attract positive people to you.

So much of what you've been working on is based on tapping into your creativity and exploring your passions. Some of you are saying to yourselves, "But I don't know what I'm passionate about!" To you I say, "Let's find out! We'll start by brainstorming!"

Get a blank sheet of paper and a pen. In the middle of the paper write your name. Draw a circle around your name.

- Now pretend you are outside of your body, looking down upon yourself. What do you see? Write it down. Use words that describe your appearance…Tall? Short? Black hair? Brunette? Blonde? Freckles? Muscular? Skinny? Fat?

- How have other people described you, your character, your personality? Charismatic? Witty? Shy? Clever? Sarcastic? Sweet? Write down everything that comes to mind, in no particular order, as long as it's on the paper.

- Next, write down everyone who is in your family. Next to their name, note their relation to you. This includes significant others and pets.

- Write down you current job, or what you do to earn a living. This can be a title or different tasks. If you are a homemaker, jot down the things you do to keep your household in order.

- What city do you live in? Include that.

 www.stephenmark.com

- Do you attend a house of worship or church? Jot that down.

- What kind of home do you live in? An apartment, duplex, home, condominium?

By now, there are lots of words staring back at you. Take a moment and draw a line from each descriptor to your circled name. All of these descriptions, people and tasks are connected to you. They are the various elements of your life.

Now turn the same paper over and begin on the other side. Think about the best day you've ever spent. Perhaps it was a family outing to the beach, or time spent at a secret hideaway. The day you met your spouse or significant other, the day you married, the birth of a child, the day you graduated from college. Reflect on the feelings you had on your special day.

Pride? Relaxation? Relief? Joy? Happiness?

Your next task is to think of things you do, or don't do actively or as a spectator, that create similar feelings inside you. Is it watching children playing? Listening to waves crash on the beach? Attending a concert? Sketching, writing, dancing or playing an instrument? Think for a few minutes and then begin writing. Don't stop writing until the words stop flowing. You've just created a list of things you are passionate about.

Looking at your list, how many on the list are you doing? Are there passions you're not currently pursuing because of time, other commitments, money, fear of failure? Think about what's keeping you from doing the things you enjoy.

Remember when you believed in Santa Claus? Can you think of what would have been on your list back then? Probably playing, building sand castles, finger painting, flying a kite, spending time with your friends or grandma and grandpa. The difference is when we were children we didn't have to make a list. We just did it. Our lives were centered on being joyful.

Let's take your list and turn it into an action plan. From all the activities on your list, choose three, the ones that you get excited about just by reading the words.

You've done this exercise enough to know what comes next:

a deadline.

A plan with no action or deadline is just a list.

Action	When	Because...
Watching the waves	Next Sunday	It's peaceful, and I deserve it
Paint	Weekly	I enjoy being creative, and I deserve it
Take French cooking lessons	Next month	I love to cook, and I deserve it

Are you seeing a pattern yet? First off, you deserve it! Secondly, these are the things that bring you joy, they nurture your soul and they are just yours. Every single person will have a very different action plan. Start small and get used to infusing your life with your passion. When practiced, it will become a habit. When you live your life with purpose and passion, you are consciously creating your life, not just going through the motions, watching life happen.

You can also use free word association to identify things you are passionate about. Finish the following sentences:

"I love it when I _____**."**

"I feel like I'm at my best when _____**."**

"I could just _____ **all day."**

"Sharing my talents with others makes me feel _____**."**

Write down the first answer that jumps into your consciousness. Think of how exciting life will feel, how absolutely fulfilled you'll be, when you start infusing passion into your every day existence.

If you can find a friend that shares your interests, buddy up with them. Set dates together to explore your passions. This is part pampering and part committing. When you make a date in your calendar, you are giving this time importance, and committing to actually doing it. Taking action to make it happen.

And money does not need to be a barrier to enjoying your passions and creating joy. The list below is just a few examples of some inexpensive ways you can take care of yourself:

Watch a sunset while sipping your favorite beverage
Rent a DVD and curl up with a blanket
Listen to your favorite CD or check out new ones for free at the library
Enjoy an afternoon sitting on the riverbank
Plant a garden
Help a neighbor with a project
Volunteer at the local animal shelter
Visit seniors at a convalescent home
Sign up for a training class of some sort

Think of how you perceive your life, as it is now. On a new sheet of paper, write down these categories:

Work

Home/Family

Community/Society

Self

Each category will act as its own heading. Under each, include important elements, for example, under "Self" you may want to include health, spirit; under "Home" you may want to include spouse, children, pets. Next rank each element on the list from zero to 10 according to its importance to you. Think of how much attention you devote to it each week and assign it a number from zero to 10. How closely do the numbers match up?

Look at the entries under each heading. What are the expectations for each from your spouse, your family, your boss? Are you meeting them? What about your own expectations? Are you meeting the standards you set for yourself?

Now your assignment and goal is to write a short narrative (story) about where you see yourself in 5 years. Think about the life you want to have and remember to use language that is alive and rich. Nothing boring here! Your narrative may be 2 paragraphs or it may be 2 pages ~ once you start writing, don't stop until you've painted a vivid picture. This is how I want you to start seeing your life, though you probably won't have to wait 5 years. Once you begin the process of allowing, creating, attracting…it starts a snowball effect.

Wow! In this chapter you've done a lot of exercises. Congratulations! My intention was to get you in touch with your passions and help you start creating and living the life you want. It's very easy to get stuck or blocked with the regular stream of negative consciousness we are exposed to on a daily basis from the news. That's why the exercises are so powerful; they force you to shift your perceptions.

It's been said that the definition of insanity is doing the same thing over and over again, and expecting different results. That's why it's important to take your life and shake it up. **Repeating negative patterns guarantees negative results.** The opposite is also true when you replace unhealthy behaviors and thoughts with new, positive behaviors and thoughts.

A dear friend of mine named Kristi was involved in a less than fulfilling romantic relationship for over a year. She was on an emotional roller coaster with her partner, and she was having a hard time getting off the ride. Her family and close confidants all tried to convince her that she was better off without the relationship, but Kristi was stuck with this partner. The good times were great; the bad times were the worst. It was difficult to watch her struggle.

One day, she shared an especially troubling episode she'd had with her boyfriend. I told her I cared for her very much. I reminded her that her relationship was the definition of insanity. She confided that she was truly unhappy, but she felt stuck. I asked her what she wanted to do about her current relationship, and told her before she answered that I didn't want her to think about it, just answer with the first thing that popped into her head. She immediately responded, "I want to break up with him." She followed by voicing her own doubt that she would be able to do it.

I asked her to do me a favor, and I will ask you to do the same. Every day when you wake up in the morning, I want you to say this to yourself:

"I care enough about myself to make a better choice."

I encouraged her to write the statement down and tape a copy to her bathroom mirror, post a copy on the steering wheel of her car and put it up in her cubicle at work.

"Look at the statement several times a day, and say it aloud. Think about it before you make any decision, no matter how small. It could be what you're going to have for lunch. Make this statement a part of your mantra. Make it something that you consider before anything else. Let it become alive in your conscious mind."

Kristi agreed. Before she attended meetings at work, she said it to herself. Before she made a telephone call, she said it. She repeated it to herself throughout the day. And before long, she started to believe it. She stopped giving her boyfriend permission to hurt her feelings or affect her in a negative way. Their connection that had been so strong, soon deteriorated and completely disappeared. Suddenly, it occurred to her that she deserved the best and she made choices that would only allow for the best.

Make sure that you care enough about yourself to make choices
that are in alignment with creating your dream life.

Chapter Seven

Barriers To Success

"Shoot for the moon – if you miss you'll end up in the stars."

– Artie Shaw

If the above is true, then go ahead and take your shot! What would you try if you knew you wouldn't fail? Think about when you were a child and believed that anything was possible. This chapter will offer resources for dealing with the barriers you may encounter on your journey.

Remember that you are in charge of your life. Through various exercises in past chapters, you've explored different ways to take care of yourself and channel your efforts in the right direction. By now, you should be visualizing your ideal life regularly. **Your transformation has already begun. Keep the momentum going and you'll continue to see results. Don't let temporary obstacles, like fear, block you from attracting good things into your life.**

Fear can be a useful emotion. It helps keep us safe. Because we don't want to get burned (we fear the pain), we wouldn't stick our hand in the fire. We take precautions in our homes, cars and offices so that we will be physically safe. People lock their cars, for fear that another person

 www.stephenmark.com

may steal their belongings or even their car. Imagine walking down a dimly lit alleyway, late at night, alone. Are your senses heightened? Do you take extra care and listen carefully for unfamiliar sounds? Your body is responding to a perceived threat, and acting accordingly.

So, at times, fear is useful. When it stands in the way of your progress, it is not.

Fear limits our ability to create, and it blocks our ability to receive.

When you expect something, you can bet it is coming. When you believe something, it is coming. When you fear something, you'll bring it into being. If there are things in your life that you no longer want to experience, you have to change your belief.

As mentioned in a previous chapter, one way to face fear head on is by taking more risks. They don't have to be huge risks, they can be calculated risks, but something outside of your comfort zone, something that will challenge you to break through the fear barrier.

Another barrier can be the pressure that other people place upon us. It could be our boss, our spouse or our family who want us to act in ways that please them. Change makes people uncomfortable. These people may criticize you or second-guess your accomplishments. Remember a few pages back when I touched on the subject of forgiveness? This is the time to forgive them.

You don't have to let them know you are doing so, but do it anyway. They are in fear and they don't feel secure. When you make changes, it's possible you might expect them to change as well. And that doesn't sound like fun, at least from their perspective. If you improve your life, will they also have to? Isn't that a lot of work? (Remember they don't have the resources you have, at least not yet – maybe you'll share this book with them or buy them a copy of their own).

Some of my loved ones are famous for laying the proverbial "guilt trip" on me. As you probably know, a guilt trip is just a form of manipulation, a way that someone attempts to get you to bend to their will. I always used to get angry with them over this, but no longer. I don't get angry, I just get clear. When I feel someone is trying to guilt me into doing something, I stop him or her and ask for clarification.

"So what you're saying is that if I do _____, it will affect you how?"

"If I don't do _____, how will that make you feel?"

"I just want to be clear that you understand, I'm choosing to do _____, because it will benefit me. Will you explain why that makes you uncomfortable?"

I use an even and calm tone of voice and make eye contact when addressing the other party. I offer them the opportunity to look at their motives. Whatever it is that I'm going to do or not going to do or think about doing…it's my choice, my action, my experience to have if I choose to do so.

The great thing about living is we all have free choice.

Sometimes we are so afraid of failure that we never even try.

Every journey begins by taking a first step.

If you don't take action, nothing happens.

If you plant a seed and never water it, you will not be able to enjoy the beautiful bloom in the spring. The techniques, tools and ideas that you are learning from this material is meant to be harvested. Let's say you visit the local book store once a month and you purchase 10 books each time. At the end of the year, you have gathered 120 books full of stories, information, prose and intellect taking up space on your shelves. If you don't open the books, none of the stories, information, prose and intellect really belongs to you.

> # If you're afraid you will fail, you'll be right.

Let's talk about what success looks like. It might not be fear of failure, but fear of success that cripples you. Think about some of the things that success brings.

Bigger paycheck

More responsibilities

Longer hours

Higher expectations

Pride

Approval from others

We expect more from people who have proven themselves to be successful. Successful people are expected to continue being successful, continue to "wow" us, and continue to overachieve. Maybe they work longer hours or maybe they accumulate more possessions. We can assume their wealth increases. You choose to either continue to move forward with the momentum you've built or you start going backwards.

I've worked with many different people who pride themselves on simply "flying under the radar" so they were not often noticed by upper management or anyone else for that fact, and therefore, not much was expected from them. That sounds a lot like settling to me. Why would I settle for living a so-so life?

Think about it? Why would you choose to settle for living a so-so life?

What are some characteristics typically used to describe "successful" people?

Ambitious ~ Driven ~ Outgoing ~ Aggressive ~ Focused

Strong work ethics ~ Dedicated ~ Personable

Intelligent ~ Worldly

Do any of those adjectives describe you or aspects of your personality? None of the characteristics above are derogatory. Could you live with it if your colleagues used any of those words to describe you? I bet you could! Play a round of the "What If" game.

What If…I believed myself to be personable?

Then I would probably be comfortable around people.

What If…I believed myself to be driven?

Then I would probably be focused on my goals.

 www.stephenmark.com

What If...I believed myself to be intelligent?

Then I would probably make choices that benefit me.

Whatever you put in motion stays in motion.

Change your beliefs to reflect the person you want to be. Don't let fear of failure stop you from trying. Remember that if you think you can't, you are always right.

Sometimes our past experiences make it difficult for us to clearly see our potential. Situations where we made mistakes or received criticism chip away at our confidence. If you can identify a situation from the past that still troubles you, I encourage you to forgive yourself. The details or circumstances of your situation do not matter. Forgiveness is a wonderful tool for releasing negative feelings and thoughts and allows us to feel lighter. Reflect on the experience and when you are ready to be rid of the negative feelings, start with your name, and say, "I forgive you." You will no longer feel the need to beat yourself up as there is no reason to. Forget the experience - remember the lesson.

Every experience offers you an opportunity for growth. A friend of mine says, "It's all good stuff, even the bad stuff!" For example, when I went out on that disaster of a blind date, the "bad stuff" was spending two hours with someone I was completely incompatible with. The "good stuff" was it enabled me to clarify the qualities I actually did want in my soul-mate. I was able to focus my intentions and start attracting what I desired.

When you are able to forgive yourself, you can forgive others. Do not hold on to old resentments or anger. **Those emotions literally block you from receiving.** If there are people in your life that you are fighting with or not speaking to, forgive them. As soon as possible – the sooner the better. When you are angry or full of conflict, you will continue to attract people or situations that bring more of the same into your life. That's not only exhausting, but also counter-productive. Apologizing may feel like taking a risk. When you take risks, you are breaking through a barrier. Forgiveness enables you to create.

Don't procrastinate!

Forgiveness is about healing you. If directly apologizing to another person would not serve your higher purpose, or put you in jeopardy, forgive them privately to yourself. Sometimes there are people in our lives who are not healthy for us to have interactions with. If contacting them to apologize would allow the possibility that you would be manipulated or abused, by all means do not make contact, but forgive them anyway. It is not necessary to directly let the other person know you are forgiving them, but I encourage you to do so when it is possible.

Certain experiences or memories are very difficult to get rid of, even after you apologize to yourself and / or others. Events related to childhood trauma can prove especially difficult. The longer we hold onto a memory, the harder it is to give it up.

If you're still troubled, write down the experience on a piece of paper and when you're done, burn it, shred it, get rid of it. You don't have to write out details of the event, just give it a name or title that makes sense to you personally. As the paper burns, visualize the negative feelings you've been carrying with you disappearing as well.

Surround yourself with a healthy support network. (If you struggle with traumatic experiences it could be beneficial to explore professional counseling or support groups). My parents used to tell me to choose my friends wisely. As a teenager I had a friend named Billie who was considered a troublemaker. His home life was fairly dysfunctional. Billie's father drank heavily to deal with his disappointments and fears. Billie was left to fend for himself quite often.

One day we went to the corner store to purchase something for Billie's father. After we paid for the items, we made our way outside and the store manager called after us. He stopped us because Billie had snuck a pack of gum into his pocket and hadn't paid for it. I was completely unaware and I certainly hadn't done anything wrong. But that didn't stop the manager from taking action. He called my parents.

I kept telling the manager, "I had nothing to do with it, really!" That's when the manager said, he believed me – he had known me for years. He knew I wouldn't steal. But because of the company I kept, assumptions were made about my character. Though the assumptions were incorrect, it was the manager's perception that I too was a thug. Guilty by association.

The realization that I was judged by the company I kept angered me. When time had passed and I had matured a bit, I realized that was an experience I could learn from. The manager had acted on his belief that like attracts like. If Billie was a thief, so was I. The manager was wrong about me being a thief, but he was right to think that like attracts like, because we draw to ourselves what we put out there. I finally understood why my parents wanted me to choose my friends wisely.

The moral of the story is to spend time with those who have qualities you admire. If you want to be a mover and shaker, surround yourselves with people who do just that. Imagine if you had a goal and enthusiasm for it. Instead of talking enthusiastically about your dreams and aspirations, you sit idly and watch television all day. You still have the goal, but you put no energy or intention into it. When you're not at home, you spend time with your best friend. They're fun, great company, and you have a lot in common, you get along great. As time goes by, your passivity continues. You and your friend still get along very well, while life keeps floating past you. Over time, your goal becomes something you mention from time to time, more like a wish really. Something you'll never have.

Yikes! Let's put the brakes on here.

Goals become just wishes if we put no energy into achieving them. You already know the most effective tool in your tool belt is creative visualization. Why in the world would you settle for watching other people's lives play out, instead of creating your own? If the company you keep settles for ho-hum, so will you.

If you need to build your support network, there are various methods for doing so. If you are by nature a gregarious outgoing person, like my sister, you can probably make friends and new acquaintances anywhere and everywhere. Years ago, my sister moved to a new town and knew only her family and a couple friends. Within a matter of months, her social calendar was filled.

My sister will talk to anyone, says hello whenever she passes a stranger on the street, and is almost always smiling. Her attitude seems to be that a stranger is just a friend she hasn't met yet. She keeps open to the possibility that every person she meets can have a positive impact on her life. But her attitude serves her life and business very well. People are drawn to my sister because she emits positive energy and is open to receiving.

Whether you have 3 friends or 300 friends is really immaterial. Who among us would not welcome making a connection with someone who could help us in our quest to create our dream life? Here's an experiment: try it - the worst-case scenario is you'll enhance your people skills; best-case scenario is you meet some amazing people who will share their gifts with you.

Over the next two weeks, each time you are at the store, library, coffee shop, wherever you go, say hello to at least one stranger. If the other person is receptive to the interaction, take it one step further and ask them "what do you do?" If you have business cards, keep some on you at all times. Introduce yourself and tell them, "I'm _____. I (sell medical devices, bake cakes, sell cars, inspect homes, wash windows, etc)." If the conversation continues, exchange business cards. This is how people and things you need come into your life.

You can also join the local chamber of commerce, either as an individual or through your business. They offer monthly meetings and opportunities for networking as well as lectures or workshops to enhance your skills. Another international organization, called BNI, is a leads networking group, where members refer potential business clients to other members of the BNI group. BNI groups can be found in nearly every major city. Often times, local non-profit agencies have openings on their boards of directors. If you have a professional skill that could be useful to the group, you may wish to become a voluntary board member and lend your expertise. You'll come in contact with other professional people with similar passions.

Universities, community centers and libraries often offer monthly lectures or classes on thousands of topics and issues. Attend the ones that interest you, and bring your business cards with you. The key to expanding your network is meeting new people. Don't sit at home saying, "I wish I could meet people." People won't find you while you're safely tucked away at home in your comfort zone. You have to get into the world to meet who's in the world.

Once you have a database of contacts, go through it regularly. Don't just collect business cards and leave them in a pile. Every week, make time to make contact with at least three people in your address book. I prefer phone calls to emails because a phone call allows for real-time interaction; however; an email is better than nothing. Make sure that your contacts know what projects you are working on, and what your goals are. You never know who knows someone who knows someone.

In the 90's, a novelty game called "Six Degrees of Kevin Bacon" hit the market. It was instantly popular with those who fondly remembered the actor from his box office smash of the early 80s, "Footloose." The game was based on the Six Degrees of Separation theory, wherein the belief is that you are only six degrees away from knowing anyone in the world. You have a friend, who has a friend, who has a friend…who knows so and so. Sometimes you're three degrees away, two degrees, six degrees, etc.

Personally, I thought the game was clever. To play the game you break into teams. Each team selects a card, which has the name of a famous Hollywood actor, producer or director. Teams huddle up and then figure out how they can get from Point A to Point B (Kevin Bacon). Say I pull a card with the name Clint Eastwood. In six degrees or less, I have to map out how Clint Eastwood knows Kevin Bacon. The team that matches their selected Hollywood personality with the least amount of degrees, wins that round. (And in case you were wondering, Clint is just one degree from Kevin, as he was the director of the movie "Mystic River" which Kevin starred in).

Think about who you know, that may know someone else that eventually somehow knows your best friend. That should get you thinking about how we all know someone who knows someone. You could use the six degrees of separation principle to reach just about anyone in the world. People support people they know.

Think of when you throw a pebble into a pond. Does it land in the water and simply sink to the bottom? Eventually it does land at the bottom, but it sends ripples along the water, doesn't it? It hits the water and actually forces the water to move and shift. Anytime we take action, we're sending out ripples in the pond.

In essence, by building your network, and accessing their gifts and talents, you're doing similar work.

Another way we sabotage our success is through procrastination. If you've spent much time around teenagers, you know they are masters of procrastination. Just ask a teenager to clean their room and two things are bound to happen: 1) they will make every excuse under the sun as to why this is not an optimal time for them to clean their room 2) they will wait until the absolute last minute to get started.

Do what you have to do,

so you can do what you want to do.

Sometimes, you just have to jump in and do it! Even those unpleasant tasks, the ones we put off until the end of the day, end of the week, or end of the month. Just because you don't give something your energy, doesn't make it go away. It leaves it untended, but it doesn't disappear and uses energy worrying about it.

In a past chapter I mentioned the fishmongers in Seattle. They have a grimy job, yet they seem cheerful and content, anxious to spread good will. While they may not always love the work they do, they choose to love the way in which they do it. That's right, choose to love the way in which they do the work. That's how you can dive in and get those things that must be done completed.

I hate housework of any kind: dusting, vacuuming, cleaning the tubs and showers. But in my household, those tasks fall to me many times. So I enjoy the way in which I do them. I put on my CDs and dance through the tasks. Sometimes I challenge myself and make it a game to finish cleaning the house in one hour or less. I firmly believe in rewarding myself when I've completed my chores, by enjoying some quiet time. When you finish a task you've been putting off, do something nice for yourself.

Who doesn't hate deadlines? We feel like we already have so much to do, and deadlines make us feel pressured and stressed. But, is stress always a bad thing? Let's take a moment to explore how stress can actually be advantageous.

Think of a beautiful pearl. How did it come to be? Technically, it started out as foreign matter that found its way inside of an oyster. Irritated, the oyster covers the foreign body and applies pressure to it, in an effort to protect itself. Eventually the pressure transforms what was once an irritant into something beautiful. That's what stress can do ~ it adds the pressure to cause transformation. Stress puts things in motion. Use deadlines to your benefit. Managing time can feel like herding cats. The trick is applying pressure to get the results you want.

Maybe your barrier is a lack of confidence. Would you believe me if I told you that many supermodels actually suffer from low self-esteem and enjoy their jobs less than the average person? Well you can trust me - it's true.

City University in London conducted a study that was recently released, concluding that models are more lonely and suspicious of others than are people employed in traditional professions. Dr. Bjorn Meyer, the lead researcher on the study, said "If your job values you solely for your looks or your ability to walk up and down, opportunities for experiencing this satisfying sense of competence may be limited."

Confidence is not guaranteed with status or position. Building your confidence is garnering the inner strength to do something and then believing in your own abilities. If there is something you need to do, just do it. The longer you procrastinate and avoid it, the more your confidence suffers. Jump in. Realize the results do not have to be perfect. When we expect perfection, we set ourselves up to be disappointed. Also realize that you are a deserving person. You deserve to have what you want.

Build your confidence through practice. Do things that confident people do. For instance, a confident person would feel right at home making a presentation to his colleagues. He knows that his colleagues respect him and believe he is knowledgeable and has information to share that will be valuable. He believes his contributions are valuable. That's because they are. Your contributions are valuable as well.

One very effective tool used by public speakers is called an anchor. The purpose of the anchor is to develop an association between a physical thing and a mental state of complete confidence.

Visualize yourself as a strong and confident being. Now think of your right hand. Your right hand symbolizes the mental state of confidence. As you are making your presentation, use small hand gestures. When you use your right hand, you are fully in your state of total confidence.

Your state of mind is linked to your anchor, in this case, your right hand.

Confident people take risks. Talk to a stranger, wear your hair differently and change your routine. Behavior becomes habit only with practice.

Affirmations are powerful ways to increase your confidence as well. Each morning, start your day by making a positive affirmation. It could be about your physical appearance, an aspect of your personality, or how you plan to experience your day. Some examples might be:

"I am a loving and gentle being."

"I see possibilities in every situation."

"I am an attractive and charismatic person."

"I have knowledge and talents to share with the world."

"Today I will make good choices."

"I will attract people and situations that bring me joy."

You are always projecting your perceptions of yourself and life, in everything that you do. The importance of the language that you use in talking to yourself and others cannot be overstated.

Maybe you think you lack the financial resources to be successful. Remember you get what you focus on, so don't focus on what you don't have, or its absence in your life will continue. How about if you shift your perception so that finances are just a detail in your life, not your main concern?

I hear people say things like, "If I had money, I would buy this and that, and then I'd feel happy." Money only has the value that we place on it. What happens when those same people get money, don't buy what they thought they would buy, and then continue to feel just as unsatisfied? Nothing has changed except some money passed through their hands. Money is not the key to happiness. On the converse, believing you don't have enough of it, is not the key to happiness either.

What is your relationship with money? Complete the following sentences:

Financial success is _____.

If I had all the money I wanted, I would _____.

My greatest problem with money is _____.

If I could change one thing about my relationship with money, I would _____.

When you limit your beliefs, you limit your wealth. Let's say you believe you have to work really hard to earn money. With that belief you will have a difficult time getting wealthy, because you believe the two are dependent on each other. Maybe you were raised to believe that money was something only powerful people had. If you don't fit into that category, then you won't have money.

Some common beliefs about money include:

Money is the root of all evil
Money isn't everything
You can't take it with you

What are some of your beliefs about money? Write down your current beliefs in one column. Next to those, write your new beliefs. Here are some examples:

"I have an abundance of wealth."
"Money comes to me easily."
"Earning money is rewarding to me."
"I can celebrate my financial independence."

Remember that changing your beliefs allows you to have new experiences. That includes experiences with money.

 www.stephenmark.com

There are two ways to have more money: spend less; make more. Spending less doesn't have to be difficult. You should be aware of where your money goes. Gather your receipts from the past month. I want you to sort them into three distinct piles.

- Pile One: **Mandatory**: expenses that were a must.

- Pile Two: **Discretionary**: optional expenses, usually related to entertainment or recreation.

- Pile Three: **Can I get the Money Back?** wild or impulse purchases.

Cut your expenses immediately by eliminating any expenses that fell into Pile Three. Examine the expenses in Pile Two and see if you can cut them in half. Use coupons and purchase products that offer rebates. Start paying attention to advertisements and make note when products you regularly purchase are on sale. Purchase private label when you can.

You might be surprised to find out what a recent study about lottery winners revealed. Researchers found that six months after winning the lottery, the winners' levels of happiness matched the levels of happiness held by people who had become paralyzed during the preceding 6 months. Imagine that. Six months after becoming incredibly wealthy, the lottery winners were as happy as paraplegics, illustrating again that money does not create happiness.

Do you feel like you don't have the appropriate level of education or training to have the life you want? Do you feel under-qualified for job opportunities? Not smart enough to be considered for promotions? Is this a belief based on facts or your perceptions? Let's say your colleague was recently promoted over you. Your first assumption is you didn't get the promotion because management decided you were not qualified. Did you apply for the promotion? Was your colleague chosen because it was a better fit with overall plans for the organization? Perhaps you weren't promoted so the opportunity best suited for you could appear later. The point is, your education, intelligence and training may not have played any part in management's decision.

If your belief is based on perception, change your perception. If it's based on facts, then consider taking classes or workshops to enhance your education and training. Your employer may even pay for your continued education, especially if it can be used in your current position or department. Investigate classes available at community colleges or the community center. If you have a lust for knowledge, satisfy it. You will be happier for pursuing a passion, and will be more marketable in the future.

Don't let the barriers you experience become larger than they are. Every problem has a solution. Successful people find creative ways to achieve their desired results.

What is currently standing in your way? Identify your **perceived barriers** and brainstorm actions you can take to eliminate them. Include a timeline or deadline for yourself. Remember what happens when the oyster applies pressure?

Obstacle/Issue	Solution	Completion Date
Don't have enough money	*Begin tracking expenses*	*March 1st*
Eliminate unnecessary expenses		
Dissatisfied w/ salary	*Talk to boss about raise*	*Feb 18th*
Enroll in a marketing course through Chamber of Commerce		
Lonely	*Visit places that interest me*	*Feb 20th*
Talk to 3 strangers, start collecting cards		

Chapter Eight

Your Personal Mission Statement

A few chapters back, I touched on the subject of creating a personal mission statement. This chapter will focus on the values and guiding principles that anchor you. Remember, you're on this journey to create a better life. This chapter will offer many exercises to help you fine-tune your clarity and focus.

You've been working on various aspects of your life and it's important to keep the momentum going. Reflect on your "Dream Board" often, it will help you when you are experiencing temporary roadblocks or feeling impatient with the process. The other exercises you've worked on are also important, and you should keep the written exercises handy. Implementing new strategies is easier when your ideas are clear, concise, and easy to apply.

Don't give up or get sidetracked from your goals. If you need something from the people around you, ask. Expect that you may experience some resistance to your changes from those around you. Stick to your boundaries, and don't take it personally if you don't receive the support you need. Make sure you have a support network in place, and align yourself with people who possess qualities you admire. And take the time to celebrate your progress and accomplishments. It's important that you take care of yourself!

Identifying your values might take some brainstorming. Below are some choices to help you get started. Select the values that resonate with you; assets or ideas that are important in your ideal life. You'll use these values as anchors when developing your personal mission statement. If you've already prepared a mission statement, that's excellent! Follow through this chapter, do the exercises and see if you want to make any modifications to your statement.

Achievement ~ Adventure ~ Aesthetics ~ Affluence ~ Autonomy
Authority ~ Balance ~ Challenge ~ Change and variety ~ Close relationships
Collaboration ~ Community ~ Competence ~ Competition ~ Courage
Creativity ~ Decisiveness ~ Democracy ~ Economic Security ~ Effectiveness
Efficiency ~ Ethical Practice ~ Excellence ~ Excitement ~ Expertise
Fame ~ Faith and Spirituality ~ Family ~ Fast-paced Work ~ Financial
Gain ~ Freedom ~ Friendship ~ Growth ~ Happiness ~ Helping Other
People ~ Helping Society Honesty ~ Humor ~ Independence ~ Influencing
Others ~ Inner harmony ~ Integrity ~ Intellectual Status ~ Involvement
Knowledge ~ Leadership ~ Love ~ Loyalty ~ Merit ~ Meaningful Work
Money ~ Order ~ Personal Development ~ Physical Fitness ~ Pleasure
Power ~ Privacy ~ Recognition ~ Reputation ~ Respect From Others
Responsibility ~ Security ~ Stability ~ Status ~ Time Freedom ~ Truth

The list isn't exhaustive, there may be things you value that aren't included, so while the list is meant to assist you, don't be limited by it. When you align your mission with your values, you begin to live your life fully.

Every successful enterprise began from a good idea. Most small businesses fold within their first year. Why do some businesses thrive and others die? Successful organizations typically study the marketplace before they open their doors. They research, plan and understand the importance of marketing. An understanding of what consumers want, where they want it, teamed with visibility, favorable reputation, effective leadership, and financial resources are key. The same principles apply as you create your ideal life.

It's time to do more homework. This exercise is designed to heighten your awareness of your competencies. The Consortium for Research on Emotional Intelligence in Organizations developed the following framework to isolate certain personality traits and competencies. After reviewing the framework, you can use the self-assessment tool to calibrate yourself. You'll be ranking yourself in the following areas:

- <u>Self-Assessment</u>: Knowing one's strengths and limits.

- <u>Self-Confidence</u>: Sureness about self-worth and capabilities.

- <u>Self-Control</u>: Managing disruptive emotions and impulses.

- <u>Trustworthiness</u>: Maintaining standards of honesty and integrity.

- <u>Conscientiousness</u>: Taking responsibility for personal performance.

- <u>Adaptability</u>: Flexibility in handling change.

- <u>Innovativeness.</u> Being comfortable/open to new ideas.

- <u>Achievement Drive</u>: Striving to improve or meet a standard of excellence.

- <u>Commitment</u>: Aligning with the goals of the group or organization.

- <u>Initiative:</u> Readiness to act on opportunities.

- <u>Optimism</u>: Persistence in pursuing goals despite obstacles and setbacks.

Self-Assessment

(F= displayed frequently, S= sometimes, I= infrequently, and R= rarely)

COMPETENCY and accompanying traits	FREQUENCY
SELF-ASSESSMENT: Aware of strengths and weaknesses; learn from experience; open to feedback.	
SELF-CONFIDENCE: Present with self-assurance; voice independent views; decisive despite uncertainties and pressures.	
SELF-CONTROL: Stay composed and positive; think clearly and stay focused under pressure.	
TRUSTWORTHINESS: Act ethically; reliable and authentic; admit mistakes and confront unethical actions; principled.	
CONSCIENTIOUSNESS: Meet commitments and keep promises; accountable; organized and careful.	
ADAPTABILITY: Smoothly handle multiple demands, shifting priorities; adapt responses to fit circumstances; flexible in perceptions.	
INNOVATIVENESS: Seek out fresh ideas from variety of sources; entertain original solutions; generate new ideas.	
ACHIEVEMENT DRIVE: Results-oriented, with a high drive to meet objectives and standards; set challenging goals and take risks; pursue information; learn how to improve performance.	
COMMITMENT: Sense of purpose in the larger mission; use values in making decisions; actively seeks out opportunities.	

 www.stephenmark.com

INITIATIVE: Ready to seize opportunities; pursue goals beyond what's expected or required.	
OPTIMISM: Persist in seeking goals despite obstacles and setbacks; operate from hope of success rather than fear of failure; see setbacks as due to manageable circumstances rather than personal flaw.	

How did you score? In which competencies do you seem to excel, and which need more attention or frequency? As you build the life you want, keep in mind which traits should receive more attention. This assessment doesn't offer a score; it's about increasing your awareness. You want your attention and intentions to be channeled in the direction that will produce the most favorable results!

During the course of reading this book, or while practicing some of the skills you're learning, you may have experienced strong reactions to certain topics. This reaction is considered a trigger. Have certain exercises been more difficult than others?

Generally a trigger goes off when your consciousness becomes aware of something you need to work on or improve. If you find yourself being triggered, take some time with the feeling and then do some analysis of the situation.

- **Triggering event:** What triggered the conflict? What was your emotional response? Do you know what your hot buttons are?

- **Perceived threat:** What did you assume was the intent behind the action that triggered you? In what ways did you feel threatened?

- **Defensiveness:** Did you feel like you needed to defend your belief system?

- **Response:** How did you respond? Can you respond differently in the future?

Exploring your values, competencies and emotional triggers should offer insight into guiding principles that will be most effective for you. Let's get to work on creating, or refining, your personal mission statement!

Everyone has heard of Microsoft and its founder, Bill Gates. When he started, Mr. Gates had an idea, a network of support, and the drive to pull it all together. Today, it's almost impossible to find a personal computer that doesn't operate on the software that carries the Microsoft label. Using our theory that it makes sense to copy what successful people do, we'll start by reviewing the Microsoft mission.

"Microsoft's mission is to enable people and businesses throughout the world to realize their full potential. One way we fulfill our mission is by developing innovative software that transforms the way people work, learn, and communicate. Another way is by using our resources and expertise to help expand social and economic opportunities in communities around the world."

Another company you're familiar with sells hot, frothy beverages in tall, short, grande and venti-sized cups with a green logo on the outside. You know who this is, there's probably at least one or twelve in your town. Starbuck's mission reads:

"Establish Starbucks as the premier purveyor of the finest coffee in the world while maintaining our uncompromising principles while we grow."

So how are they doing? Are these two companies guided by the principles and values defined in their mission statements? Their respective successes and philanthropic corporate programs suggest that they are. This is a process and you may need to do some more brainstorming or make multiple attempts before you're satisfied with yours. Try to keep it simple, between 3-5 sentences. If it's too complicated, the focus can get lost. The samples below may help you get started:

"My mission is to achieve financial abundance and share my wealth and knowledge with others in my community who may need assistance. I will use my special talents to better myself and my family and celebrate the achievements of my loved ones."

"I will act with compassion and mentor those in my life, offering them support, love and praise, to help them become productive and caring citizens. I will actively seek out opportunities to learn and will share my knowledge with others. I will meet each day with gratitude and a sense of promise."

"My mission is to listen to my intuition, act with confidence, and experience joy and love in all my relationships. I will focus my energies on achieving good health and spiritual awareness."

When your statement is ready, write it out and put it in places you will see it, and see it often. Remember the saying, "I care enough about myself to make a better choice?" I asked Kristi to post the saying in her cubicle, on her mirror; in her car…this is the same thing you'll do with your mission statement. You can personalize your email signature to include your mission statement; you want to get the word out. Share it with your friends and your significant other. You will attract whatever you focus your attention on, so be prepared!

Another saying I want you to keep in mind during your process of transformation is "If you want the rainbow, you've got to put up with a little rain." Country western singer Dolly Parton said it, and I think it's profound, and in my experience, it's true. When you share your mission statement, you may not receive the reaction or support from others that you expected. Don't let it deter you. This process is about you! Your mission statement and the daily affirmations, these are all tools meant to keep you on track. And your boundaries are in place so that you will remain emotionally safe. If you seek validation or approval from outside sources, you may be disappointed. Remember that your feelings, your thoughts, your aspirations are all valid.

Keep going!

What you set in motion stays in motion.

My friends are a rather mixed group of personalities; every one is truly an individual. We also have a lot in common, after all, that is what attracted us to each other. In our group, Gary could be called the "doubter." You've heard of looking for the silver lining? Gary will tell you that inside of your silver lining is an even bigger black lining and you'll never break through it to see the sun and even if you did, the sun causes cancer, and then... Optimism doesn't come naturally to Gary, but he's working on it. When I shared my personal mission statement with Gary, he listened, smiled and said, "Huh. So where are we going for lunch?" Ah, Gary. Fortunately, I am not a person who seeks my validation from others, because if I did, I would have been crushed by his response, or rather I should say lack of response.

Your mission statement is like a preface to your road map. It guides you in your life and the choices that you make. As your life changes and progresses, your mission may or may not shift. Maybe your mission will guide you for the next 6 months, or perhaps longer. There is no magic number or expiration date. It works as long as it works for you, and keeps you moving forward. Remember that you believe whatever you tell yourself. Use your affirmations and mission statement to transform the way you view yourself and your life.

Think about when children play "pretend."

Here's more homework for you...visualize your perfect life. What do you look like? Who are you spending your time with? Where do you live? Do you work, and if so, doing what? Do you have a family? How

---

do you spend your leisure time? If you did the Dream Board assignment, you have a prop prominently displayed and your perfect life is already collaged. This time, I want you to spend some time writing a journal entry. In this entry, write about the perfect day you just spent in your ideal life. Describe everything that happened during your perfect day. Use language that suggests the ideal life is happening right now. Your entry could begin like this:

"Today I spent the most marvelous day _____!

_____ and _____ were with me and we _____..."

Keep writing until you run out of words.

When you meditate, envision what you wrote in your journal entry as if watching a movie of your perfect day. Your clarity and focus should be very sharp now, and you will begin attracting people and situations that will open doors or present opportunities for you to get closer to your ideal life.

In the next chapter, we'll cover how you can be even more proactive in building the life you want.

Part Three

Taking Action,

Right Now

Chapter Nine

If You Don't Do Anything,
You Won't Get Anywhere

I have a philosophy, "When "it" quits being fun, quit doing it." I changed jobs often when I was younger. The idea has merit; it's the application that matters. If "it" happens to be a new relationship, a hobby or an activity that is meant to be leisure and enjoyable, but becomes a chore - change it and find something enjoyable. But if you ever want to leave the driveway, you have to put the car in drive. Let's rev up the engines and get going!

Like the song lyrics in "Live Like You Were Dying" by Tim McGraw, "Live like you were dying, love deeper, spoke sweeter, gave forgiveness I've been denying, like tomorrow was a gift, and you got eternity to think about what you did with it." If we could all focus our energies on what is important to our life, our goals, our mission, we could move beyond the anger, the pain, the hate and rise above it all creating a life of abundance, your dream life.

You've spent the past several chapters exploring your values, belief systems, perceptions and barriers. The law of attraction aids your focus

     www.stephenmark.com

and intentions and you create opportunities in your life when you make the space to receive. That's the groundwork.

Life is not a passive activity, and hoping for the best isn't going to be enough. First, make sure that you are paying attention to the opportunities that already exist around you. If you have tunnel vision or wear blinders, you miss the activities going on around you. Focus, while remaining open.

Something you can do immediately is listen to the conversations taking place around you. Everyday you have two choices. 1) Inertia: the tendency of bodies at rest to stay at rest; 2) Momentum: the tendency of bodies in motion to remain in motion. Which one will you need to create your ideal life? If you're having a tough time getting in gear, enlist the help of a friend or a life coach. When you have someone cheering you on, sometimes kicking you off the couch or out of a slump, it's impossible to ignore. Think of how wonderful it would be to have your own personal cheerleader pushing you, motivating you! Each step you take to make things happen in your life is a big one. What if you heard applause every time you took a step?

We're taught at a young age that putting ourselves first makes us self-centered. That's literally the definition of selfish and it's not an adjective that we want attached to our name. But, if we don't put ourselves first, that means we are putting others ahead of ourselves. Think of what a disaster that would be in an emergency? Why is it when you ride on a commercial airline, the stewardess goes over the emergency procedures, he or she instructs you to affix your own air mask before helping anyone else? You can't be well enough to care for others if you're not caring for yourself. This is the time to put you first.

In order to do so, you need to delegate your tasks and obligations to others whenever possible. You can't be all things to all people. Delegating is setting a boundary, an expectation that someone other than you will handle a task. Ask them. One of the most important tasks that new managers learn is the skill of delegating to their subordinates. We all get 24 hours each day, you can't manufacture more time, but you can borrow someone else's skills or talents to get things done. Right?

When I ask you to put yourself first and be selfish, I'm not advising you to be dispassionate or dishonorable. If you notice an elderly woman who needs help finding her car, by all means be generous with your time. If someone asks you for charity, be generous with your gift. (By the way, giving to others makes you feel better, so it's a selfish way of being unselfish!) Being selfish could be a new behavior, but I urge you to allow yourself to start telling others "no" and putting you first.

In fact, start giving things away that you can spare or part with. Be generous with everything you can spare, including change, clothes, furniture, your time...what you give back returns to you, but in a different form. Give away smiles. Put coins in the parking meter of a stranger. Leave the waiter an extra $5 on top of a fair tip. To have the new, you move out the old. Generate good will; you will get it back in return. Volunteer, visit the elderly, mentor a child, call a sick friend or give the neighbor's dog a biscuit. You are constantly putting off energy that others are attracted to. Negative attracts negative; positive attracts positive. Take an active approach to creating good will and be ready. It's on the way.

Make your network work for you. Call at least one person every day. Before you decide that you're too busy, this only needs to take five minutes or so. If you're pressed for time, simply tell the other party at the beginning of the call you only have a few minutes. Share stories and listen. If they have a gift, contact or opportunity that can help you, ask them. Contacting someone every day will create the habit of telling your story, asking for what you want, connecting with others and keep up your momentum. As this gets easier for you, increase the number of contacts you make each day. Remember the Kevin Bacon game? Yes, this is a little like that. You never know who knows someone, who knows someone...you get the idea.

Be aware of your communications with others and yourself.

Talk the talk of a winner. You will be more positive to be around and you'll attract others.

When you wake up in the morning, or if you prefer, before you go to bed for the night, figure out what is most important about tomorrow. Write down what must get done. Review your list when you begin your day. Cross off the task when it's completed. It feels good to cross something off the to-do list. It's evidence of your accomplishment, right in your hands.

Write down what you want, 15 times each day. Yes, another list. This tool is extremely effective. Again, you have to do more than think happy thoughts and talk about it. Don't just dream: DO. Thomas Edison said, "If we did all the things we were capable of, we would literally astound ourselves."

Experience is an excellent teacher.

We figure out what not to do anymore.

Remember the definition of insanity? Keep doing things the same way, again and again, and expect the results to be different. That's insanity. Shift your beliefs and allow for other possibilities and you'll experience something new.

I also encourage you to look for your own responsibility when you have an unpleasant experience or exchange with someone. Questions to consider:

- **Did I take something personally?**
- **Am I trying to interpret something that doesn't need interpreting?**
- **Could I have responded in a different way?**
- **Was I acting in a manner consistent with serving my greater purpose?**
- **What would a more positive outcome of the situation look like?**

- **What, if anything, could I do to avoid a similar experience in the future?**
- **Can I forgive myself and others involved in this situation?**

There are always opportunities for you to analyze your behaviors. We are unable to control others, their reactions and their inactions. We don't control situations, but we don't have to let situations control us either. **You control your reaction to people and your environment.** You can choose to see a situation or experience any way you wish. Reflect on the experience, examine your own reactions and behaviors and reframe it so you will not repeat the unpleasant situations and will attract the positive. Forgive when necessary, beginning with yourself.

Knowing you can only control your actions and reactions, when someone else does something, is it your business? Sure, their behavior can have an impact on you, it will have whatever impact you decide.

Life is a lot like going to school. You can't just show up and expect to get good grades. Sure recess is fun and you get to socialize and you can even learn. But what if you don't do the work? You could just stay in bed all day and have the same result. So get into your life. Take charge. Decide what you will do, when and get it done.

If you knew you only had one day left of your life, at your current age, in your current situation, what would you do with that last day? Live every day like it's the only one you have. Because truly, what more do we have than what we experience in this moment? Your attitude colors how you experience all your moments. Start living in the moment – you'll be amazed at how free you will feel.

Let's say one of your goals is to attract a loving relationship. Are you making an attempt to meet people? Engage in activities that you enjoy or find stimulating. Say hello to strangers. Meet people who like the things that you enjoy. Use creative visualization to create your perfect partner into being. Of course, Mr. or Ms. Right isn't going to materialize on your front doorstep, you'll have to do some work. You can't find them when you're overcome with loneliness, sitting on your couch, complaining into the phone to your friends, "I'll never meet the ONE." Not unless he or she is dropping by random houses, knocking on doors, looking for you. And unless you're a character in a television series or movie, it's probably not going to happen like that.

You've been working on your goals and doing exercises all through this book. Yes, it's a lot of work. It's like reprogramming yourself to release the negative and receive the positive. To see things how you want them to be.

By now you have many tools at your disposal and you've learned some tips to keep you on track. You should be able to do this next task very easily.

Make a list of all the things you need to DO, actions you need to take, to have your ideal life. Include the date you will DO the action by. The rule is, you MUST do at least ONE thing EVERY day. Start creating your new dream life, now.

Tasks	Date
Examine monthly spending; determine what can be eliminated or where spending can be reduced	Jan. 30
Call one person each day, starting with Sarah	Jan. 31
Research and sign-up for online computer class to improve skills and be eligible for next quarter promotion	Feb. 1

(Your list should be a long one! And you will check off one thing each day! This list can change, be added to, modified in ways to create your dream life.)

Chapter Ten

Living With Change As An Ever-Present Factor In Your Life

Sometimes I'm not convinced my dog understands she's is a dog. She insists on spending her sleeping hours sprawled out on the couch, her waking hours trying to charm anyone who comes to visit into giving her a treat or a belly rub, and other times attempting to convince us she is in control of the home. She isn't limited by her small physical body size, she just is. She eats, sleeps, communicates and is self-assured. If she wants something, she goes for it and doesn't give up. If it means rousing her from a nap or interrupting her bliss, she ignores it. When she needs something, she lets me know. Somehow she has it all figured out. She just is. Her life is simple and she takes each day as it comes, seemingly unconcerned what may happen in the next moment.

I tell my wife, "our dog doesn't know she's a dog." I wonder what would happen if it occurred to her that she was a dog? Would she then act accordingly? Would she change her behaviors to conform to an idea of what a dog should be? Who would set the stage for these new behaviors? Hmmm…

 www.stephenmark.com

How would you live **your** life if you felt unbound by constraints, ignoring the labels that others place on you? What would happen if you refused to be limited? What would happen if you didn't care so much about what others were saying about you, or how they were looking at you?

What does my dog have to do with all this, the work of changing your life? I want you to remember to pay attention to those who appear successful and living their bliss. They don't spend time fearing the unknown or lamenting about the dreams they don't think they will realize.

If you change just one perception, you will feel different, immediately. Take for instance when you have a tough morning. Let's say your alarm didn't wake you, which causes you to rush, for fear of being late. Your body is tight with stress, you feel irritated and a sense of panic. Jogging to the car, you spill your coffee down the front of your shirt. Just what you needed! Over and over, you lament on what an awful day you're having. "What else could possibly happen?!" you wonder aloud, through clenched teeth.

The Universe hears, "I want more experiences to convince me I am having a terrible morning." The Universe recognizes your intention, your desire and delivers what you ask for. So, on the way into the office, you're in a snarl of traffic making you even later. Exasperated, you can't believe your bad fortune. You are never going to make it to the 8:30 meeting, you keep telling yourself. And you're right; you don't make it to the meeting on time.

Is this the time for a meltdown? There is a right answer to this question.

Let's experience the morning through a different filter, a different perception. The alarm didn't go off and you may be late for your commitments at the office. Things happen. Call the office and leave a message and then let it go. If you run around in a state of chaos and panic, you'll attract more chaos. Prepare yourself for the day with intention.

On the way to the car, your coffee spills and your outfit is now stained. How fortunate that you purchased laundry detergent and a cleaning stick when you were at the store the other day. As you sit in traffic, you pass the scene of the car accident that had taken place only a few minutes prior. Had you been on time this particular morning, perhaps your car would have been on the road at the exact time of the accident, and could it have been you? Thankfully, you left the house just a few minutes later than usual. The disruption to your routine might have spared you a real emergency.

Don't allow the small stuff to become the big stuff. When you feel as though you are having a bad day, stop yourself and take a quick inventory. Ask yourself:

- *Is this really as bad as I'm making it?*

- *Is my mood perpetuating more negative things?*

- *Am I telling the Universe I want more of this, because it's what I'm focusing on?*

What you set in motion stays in motion. Be intentional with your thoughts and perceptions. You control your reactions and perceptions, <u>not the mitigating issue.</u>

As you make changes in your life, more change will come. Additional opportunities will be created and attracted to you. There are always forces at work to help you create your reality. Sometimes we grow impatient, which causes us to lose our focus or shift to negativity.

Getting the things you want may not happen overnight or instantly. If that were true, wouldn't everyone be rich, in love, successful and completely content?

What does happen instantly when you shift a perception, you begin to attract what you want. Replacing a negative feeling with a positive feeling can happen right now, in this moment. The work we struggle with is keeping things in motion. That is why you cannot be passive during the process of creating your ideal life. If you become frustrated, step back and regroup. The law of attraction is always working.

My point here is that as you begin to change your life, your wants and desires will shift, too. This doesn't mean you made a mistake or the Universe sent you the "wrong" thing or opportunity. Keeping in mind that each experience is one you can learn from, how can any experience be a mistake?

Let's say you want more friends. Be a better friend. Email and call your friends often. Tell them they are important to you and you are grateful that they are in your life. What happens when you do this? Your email inbox fills up and your phone starts to ring. You feel an abundance of friendship.

I enjoy the creative process and from the time I was young, I wanted to be an Entrepreneur, a coach, a motivator. Every time I had an amazing or unusual experience, I would think to myself, "I should write about that." I would have another amazing experience and say "I should write about that." I became a collector of unique and interesting experiences, and the pages stayed blank.

What a simple concept.

Be what you aspire to be.

As we've discussed, **change is a funny thing. Most of us resist it,** because it means we have to do things differently, get out of the routine, step out of our comfort zone and learn new habits, new ways of operating. Learn. Change. Adapt. Transform. Dream. Create. These aren't passive states of being, they are actions. A good friend of mine always told me, "Life isn't a dress rehearsal. Get on stage." Historian, playwright and social activist Howard Zinn wrote a book entitled *You Can't Be Neutral On a Moving Train.* Think about that for a moment…once the train has left the station you have to decide, are you going to stay on board or get off? There's no place for indecision.

YOUR LIFE IS HAPPENING RIGHT NOW!

When you experience changes in your life, take note of your reactions.

Are you afraid?

Does it feel foreign?

Are you feeling insecure?

What are the benefits of this change?

What affect does it have on your life?

Journal your emotions and reactions to change. Pull the "worst case scenario" or "what if" tools out of your toolbox as you need them. What is the worst thing this change will bring? What is the best thing that will happen? Change creates more change.

Change can mean giving up something, like a behavior or an addiction. I urge you to take an inventory of your current attitudes, behaviors and addictions. If you currently have habits that are detrimental to your physical being, like smoking, overindulgence with food, alcohol or drugs, realize that your life will be richer when you are operating without these crutches. You can experience an enriching life and have joy, by creating it. Now think of the limits your addictions and current behaviors put on you. Freedom from the things that limit you will allow your amazing potential to increase infinitely. If you are not taking proper care of yourself, you cannot fully share your gifts with others in your life.

In my mind, change isn't as difficult. The challenge is getting it to stick. It takes at least 21 days for a thought or idea to become a new belief. I don't mean to negate the idea that you can make changes right in this moment. You can create change now. But for something to become a habit, something that comes naturally and without effort, it takes persistence. Not forever.

When you think of 21 days, that's only three weeks. It has to be three weeks of repetition and persistence though. You will not create a new habit by thinking of it once and then dismissing it. How easy would that be? Perhaps a little scary as well. If every random or passing thought was creating your life, your life would be rather chaotic, wouldn't it?

Your random thoughts don't shape your life, so don't feel as though you can never have a moment of doubt, anger, irritation or sadness. I have my ups and downs due to my debilitating migraines. You create things when you apply intention to thought. Life doesn't happen by accident. It's a process of intentional creation. You can shift your mood in an instant by thinking of something that gives you joy. You can't create your perfect relationship by simply thinking, "It would be great to wake up with Jessica Alba or Jennifer Anniston." Trust me, it's better this way. If you could create by accident, you would be on a constant roller coaster.

When an organization makes changes, the company experiences a process known as "organizational transformation." There are countless experts in the field and businesses focused on helping companies to move their employees through change. The experts offer tools and insights designed to enable the employees to embrace the new business principles and stay positive and productive throughout the process. The process of changing your life is similar to the process used by companies who undergo restructuring.

One of the first techniques involved in organizational transformation is gaining an understanding of the employees current belief system. From the employee perspective:

- **What are the benefits of maintaining the status quo?**

- **In what ways will the proposed change affect the employee directly?**

- **How will it change the ways in which the employees conduct business?**

- **Are these changes positive or negative? How so?**

The bottom line people want to know is, "how will this affect me?" Let's look at why the employees have a vested interest in the outcome.

There are many competitors in the marketplace

Consumers have changing needs and interests

Keeping their jobs means continued compensation

Improving their skill set makes them marketable in future career opportunities

Efficiency or improved systems may ease their workloads

These employees have the opportunity to learn new methods of doing business that may in the end improve their ability to generate revenue, solidify their company's position in the marketplace, learn new skills and improve their overall job satisfaction. There are incentives attached to the outcome of the process.

    www.stephenmark.com

And so it is with your own restructuring. There are tangible benefits to doing things differently. When you envision how your changes will improve your life and make you feel more fulfilled, there really is no doubt that change is a good thing, is there?

When companies restructure, they don't do so simply because Mike from the mailroom had a good idea. They conduct research, they analyze the current methods and they make projections on how the restructure will impact the company's profitability. Oftentimes they hire experts to assist them in the implementation of the changes. I encourage you to do the same.

Maybe you want to get in shape, live in a healthier body. Consider joining the gym, finding a workout buddy to keep you motivated, commit the time in your day planner and meet with a professional trainer. Personal trainers are available at most gyms and depending on how much of your financial resources you wish to invest, you can meet with them daily, weekly or twice a month. Who knows, maybe your friend or neighbor is a trainer? Perhaps you can meet with the trainer once or twice, have them show you the workout techniques and once you feel comfortable, do them on your own.

Maybe you want to look fabulous and you want to change your hairstyle. Invest in a professional. Don't stand in front of the mirror when you're having a bad hair day and take matters into your own hands. If you don't have the right tools or skills, find them, obtain them, learn them. Pay someone who has the knowledge to deliver the service you desire. Make an investment in yourself. You are your most valuable asset.

If you want to make a career change, but don't know where to begin, contact a career counselor or professional coach. Or talk to someone who is currently employed in the field you are interested in. Ask questions, and find out the steps they took to build their career. Professionals can assist you in assessing your strengths, interests and help you work through your phone book. They can help you to recognize opportunities you may have previously overlooked.

The process doesn't stop once you've become successful. Imagine an Olympic athlete. Do you think after they have won the gold medal they simply say, "Ok, that's done. I've achieved my goal. There is nothing left for me to do." It's unlikely. They have succeeded, and through their efforts, have developed the mindset of a winner. Many go on to share their gifts with others and coach aspiring athletes. And they set new goals.

Imagine yourself as the gold medal Olympic athlete. You have the attitude of a winner. You go after what you desire and experience success. And you continue to attract more success. Think like the winner you are and think of five things you would like to accomplish within the next five years. Maybe one of your goals is to attend law school, start a family, travel abroad, pay off that debt or create a rainy day savings account. Envision how achieving these goals will enhance your life. Imagine how it will positively impact your family and those you care about.

Whatever your top five goals are, write them down. What actions will you take to ensure your success? What will you do to make these goals real?

Are you creating a list or an action plan?
A plan with no action is just a list.

Within the next five years, I will ….

_____

and it will benefit my life in the following ways:

_____

it will benefit my family and friends in the following ways:

_____

And so on…

Remember that focusing on what you want and using creative visualization are two of the most effective tools in your toolbox. What would you attempt if you knew you could not fail?

Part Four

It's great to see you got this far!!

CONGRATULATIONS!

Welcome To Your New Life

How do you feel? You have come on quite a journey in this book and I imagine that some of you are still trying to process some of the wonderful things you have learned that will help you live the life you want. Let's briefly recap what you have learned. In Chapter One you learned about perceptions and why it was possible for you to be a success by changing your mind about what success was all about. In Chapter Two, we continued this theme and considered how we measure success. You were introduced to some famous people who had achieved their success and we discussed how it might be possible we are already a success and just didn't know it.

In Chapter Three, you were asked to think about who has control over your life and I imagine some of you were surprised with the answers you found. Most of us have been influenced by other people at some point or another in our lives, but to be truly happy and healthy, we need to be living our life the way we want to; not in accordance with somebody else. Then in Chapter Four, we moved on to methods we could use to help ourselves, such as using "what if" techniques, "the worst case scenario" and logical thinking patterns. You were also introduced to the importance of focus in your life.

     www.stephenmark.com

Chapter Five had you asking the question "what do I really want" and you found out this was not an easy question to answer. You also learned the important lesson of the difference between "wants" and "shoulds." Chapter Six expanded this thought and encouraged you to think about things you could do and what things in life made you feel good. Chapter Seven had you addressing some of the barriers you might be putting up yourself: thereby sabotaging your own path to success. By Chapter Eight, you were working on your personal mission statement and working out what is important in your life right now.

Then we moved to the action part of the book. In Chapter Nine, we explored the simplistic statement "if you don't do anything, you won't get anywhere" and you read about the importance of action. It doesn't matter how connected to the Universe you are – you still need to take action to make your dreams come true. Chapter Ten had us looking at the whole concept of change and provided you some tips on how change can be a positive experience in your life. You also learned some basic tools to start planning and creating your own dream life.

Our lives are a continuous journey from the first breath we take until the last. It is up to us as individuals to create lives for ourselves that are productive, fulfilling and above all, happy. If you are unhappy in any area of your life, you owe it to yourself to make the changes you need to be happy again. You have the tools, now keep creating, keep dreaming…

You deserve nothing less, so make a commitment towards your happier, healthier self,

TODAY.

RIGHT NOW!

We'd love to hear from you...

How did this book help you?

How did this book change your life?

Did you choose to make changes to better your life?

Please send any feedback or comments to:

Dream Board Publications LLC
1353 Riverstone Parkway
Suite 120-252
Canton, GA 30114

Or visit our website:

http://www.stephenmark.com

or

http://www.dreamboardpublications.com

Appendix

Test and Worksheet Exercises

How Happy Are You?

First, something easy – let's see how happy you are. Just circle the response you feel most suits you to the five questions below.

1. I feel my life is pretty good at this point in time						
Strongly Disagree	**Disagree**	**Slightly Disagree**	**Neutral**	**Slightly Agree**	**Agree**	**Strongly Agree**
1	2	3	4	5	6	7
2. I am happy with my home and work situation						
1	2	3	4	5	6	7
3. I feel good about myself and my life						
1	2	3	4	5	6	7
4. I am working on things that are important in my life						
1	2	3	4	5	6	7
5. I don't regret anything I have done so far in my life						
1	2	3	4	5	6	7

This is an easy test to score, simply add up the total of the numbers you have circled. Write your score down here _____. Now we can see briefly what these numbers mean.

If you scored **between 5 and 14**, this indicates you don't feel very happy in your life and you are probably living your life in accordance with other people, and you are not getting what you want in your life in any area including friendships, intimate relationships, work prospects, or leisure activities.

If you scored **between 15 – 25** you have your good moments. If your scored in this range, you should be able to identify some areas of your life that are making you happy, and through the process of elimination, be able to see areas of your life that need changing.

If you scored **between 26 – 31** you are, for the most part, a happy person. You obviously have a good sense of humor, like to go out and have some fun and you are more likely to view positive aspects about other people, rather than their negative traits. You can still increase your happiness, but all in all you are doing fine.

If you managed to get a score **between 31 and 35** you couldn't be any happier than you are right now. While that is really good in terms of enjoying your life and taking on new experiences, if you still don't feel you are very successful, then there must still be some area of your life that this brief test did not cover, or you are not admitting the problem to yourself.

    www.stephenmark.com

Attitude and Moods

Ok, now we are going to look at your attitude and mood throughout the day.

This test is a little longer than the other one, there are thirty questions in all, but it is a good idea to answer them all so you can get a clear indication of how happy you are in practice on a day-to-day basis:

1. I find something to laugh at in life everyday			
Strongly Disagree 1	2	3	**Strongly Agree** 4
2. I prefer people to be factual and unemotional when talking to me			
1	2	3	4
3. I often have sad days			
1	2	3	4
4. I find it easy to relax in positive surroundings			
1	2	3	4
5. I believe work comes before any leisure time			
1	2	3	4
6. I often feel irritable or bitter			
1	2	3	4
7. I find a silver lining in every cloud			
1	2	3	4
8. I consider myself an academic person			
1	2	3	4
9. I don't like it if I am being quiet and my friends insist on trying to make me feel better			
1	2	3	4
10. I am usually wearing a smile on my face			
1	2	3	4
11. I prefer to weigh things up carefully and write up lists of the pros and cons of any decision I have to make			
1	2	3	4

12. I do have bad days when I think I should have stayed in bed			
1	2	3	4

13. I am usually happy			
1	2	3	4

14. I search for the facts in a situation, and treat them seriously			
1	2	3	4

15. Sometimes I feel bad tempered for no apparent reason at all			
1	2	3	4

16. I find that laughter lifts my mood as well as others, so I laugh a lot			
1	2	3	4

17. I prefer serious conversations to people being silly			
1	2	3	4

18. Sometimes I can be in a good mood			
1	2	3	4

19. I feel at peace when surrounded by happy people			
1	2	3	4

20. I would rather watch serious programs like documentaries, than fun programs			
1	2	3	4

21. I have more "blue" days than good ones			
1	2	3	4

22. If other people laugh around me, I start laughing too			
1	2	3	4

23. I like to help other people or do chores when I have some spare time			
1	2	3	4

24. There are some days when I am so depressed nothing can bring me out of it			
1	2	3	4

25. I am basically a happy person			
1	2	3	4

26. I fill my days with important appointments and work commitments			
1	2	3	4

27. If someone is acting silly around me, they can put me in a bad mood			
1	2	3	4

28. I love making other people laugh			
1	2	3	4

 www.stephenmark.com

29. I sometimes think my friends just want to have fun and nothing else			
1	2	3	4
30. Sometimes my "bad" days can last more than the one day			
1	2	3	4

To score this test you need to complete the following table. You will see that the test measures three different types of personality variables and that the questions you answered fall under one of three categories. To find out your score, simply write your numerical answer to each question in the table and then add up the columns. This will give you three separate scores concerning your attitudes and moods.

Being Happy		Being Serious		Being in a Bad Mood	
Question Number	Your Score	Question Number	Your Score	Question Number	Your Score
1		2		3	
4		5		6	
7		8		9	
10		11		12	
13		14		15	
16		17		18	
19		20		21	
22		23		24	
25		26		27	
28		29		30	
Your score		**Your score**		**Your score**	

Being Happy

If your score in the first column is **less than 27**, you are a very glum person. If you scored **between 28 and 30,** you could be considered gloomy as opposed to glum, but still not very happy. The issue with both of these scores is that you might have a tendency to hang on to petty concerns and problems. This can be a problem for two reasons: 1) the stress of carrying around the accumulated baggage you have could kill you and 2) the more petty worries you accumulate, the deeper the negative filter you view life through will become – which will result in more negativity.

Lighten up a bit and learn to let things go once in a while.

If you scored **between 31 and 34**, you could be called a glad person and if you **scored 35 to 37,** you could be considered bright and perky. If you have scored in either of these two ranges you are one of life's happier people, which is a really great way to be. You might not always be aware of problems around you and on the odd occasion you might hurt your friend if you tried to share your view of his or her problems with him or her, but basically you are a great person to be around, especially at a party.

If your score was **higher than 38,** Congratulations! You are a very happy person and you obviously take your life in stride. You are not as likely to be impacted by illness caused by stress and you have enough self esteem to keep you going through some of the most difficult situations life has to offer. Share your good humor with others.

Being Serious

This section was to find out if you thought things were funny (when they weren't) or if you have a more solemn outlook on life than people around you. If you *scored* **22 or less,** you consider most of the world is just too serious by half and you don't want to be a part of that. Just be careful that your love of pranks and jokes don't alienate you from your more serious friends.

If you scored *from* **23 to 27,** you do think about things quite seriously and you are not likely to join into silly things. You still have the capacity to have fun, which is a good thing, because if you scored in this range you are averagely serious which is a good balance to be.

If you scored from **28 or more,** you are in a position where you just want life to be serious all the time and you have no time for any fun. People with this type of score are often workaholics, or spend all their time in academic pursuits. I am not suggesting for a minute that this is a bad thing, but you might want to try going out socially once in a while, or relaxing at the beach.

Being in a Bad Mood

This is the test that most people feel uncomfortable being honest with. None of us wants to be seen as controlling or irritable, or that we might have a temper problem. But honest acceptance of yourself can only occur through honest analysis, so if you think you might have fudged the test just a little bit, go back and change the scores to be a better reflection of who you are inside.

If you had a low score in this section of the test **16 or less,** you are the type of person who just doesn't let things get you down. You are usually in a good mood all of the time and you are able to handle any potential problems with a bit of tact and grace, which is a good thing. You are a very peaceful person to be around. If you score is a little higher, **between 17 and 21,** you are a pretty typical person. You do have some bad days, but not often and usually only when something particularly annoying or problematic springs up in your face.

If you *scored* **22 or higher** on this part of the test, you might want to think about changing your life, because it would appear that you have to struggle with every aspect of your life. The path through our lives is meant to have a few bumps in it, but we are not meant to fight so hard just to maintain the status quo. If you have scored highly here, this book will be helpful to you in terms of finding out the source of your bad mood and unhappiness, changing your life for the better.

The Peak Experiences Test

The next test is designed to find out what type of event or experience you associate with the happiest times in your life. Some of the more common times we feel this way is if we have just witnessed the birth of a child (or had one), wedding days are another common high point in life, vacations, so to is graduating from college. Some of us get a lot of pleasure from taking a walk in a park or place of natural beauty, while the more physical among us may get the same pleasure from bungee jumping or white water rafting. Research has shown that there are nine "peak experience types"; that is experiences that we can have that will give us the most pleasure. These nine types of experiences are defined in the table below.

The Nine Peak Experiences	
Peak Type	**Peak Experience Examples**
Social	Having fun with other people
Artistic	Enjoying or creating art, music or literary works
Athletic	Playing the game, excelling at what you do
Nature	Feeling a oneness with the power of nature
Sexual	The feeling of togetherness that comes from intimacy
Altruistic	The high you get when you help other people
Chemical	The high you can get from drugs
Academic	The pleasure that can come from learning
Political	The excitement that comes from putting your ideas into action

          www.stephenmark.com

This test format is true and false statements. Statement starters are listed at the top of two columns. Statement endings are listed below. Make sure you read the top of the column before you read the statement below it. Then answer "True" or "False" as to whether or not that full statement applies to you. Once again, remember there are no right or wrong answers here; you are just trying to understand what type of experiences you have had through your life.

I have had an experience that made me extremely happy, and at least temporarily...		I have never had an experience that made me extremely happy and at least temporarily...	
1. Made me feel more unique than I usually feel	T/F	2. Removed much of my perplexity and confusion	T/F
3. Caused me to feel that the world was sacred	T/F	4. Moved me closer to a perfect identity	T/F
5. Caused my private, selfish concerns to fade away	T/F	6. Helped me to totally accept the world	T/F
7. Gave my whole life new meaning	T/F	8. Made me want to do something good for the world	T/F
9. Caused time to seem to stand still	T/F	10. Made me feel very lucky and fortunate	T/F
11. Caused me to feel great kindness towards humanity	T/F	12. Made me feel as if all my wants and needs were satisfied	T/F
13. Caused me to like and accept everyone	T/F	14. Allowed me to realize that everyone has his/her place in the universe	T/F
15. Caused me to feel that the world is totally good	T/F	16. Made me accepting of pain that I usually am in	T/F
17. Caused me to become disorientated in time	T/F	18. Made me feel both proud and humble at the same time	T/F
19. Removed many of my inhibitions	T/F	20. Gave me a sense of obligation to do constructive things	T/F

I <u>have had</u> an experience that made me extremely happy, and at least temporarily…		I <u>have never</u> had an experience that made me extremely happy and at least temporarily…	
21. Made me feel freer than I usually feel	T/F	22. Involved total listening	T/F
23. Made me very grateful for the privilege of having had it	T/F	24. Gave my life new worth	T/F
25. Made me feel as if I had everything, I could not think of anything else that I wanted	T/F	26. Caused me to feel that the world is totally beautiful	T/F
27. Reduced my anxiety level greatly	T/F	28. Helped me to appreciate beauty to a greater degree than I usually do	T/F
29. Caused me to believe that I could not be disappointed by anyone	T/F	30. Put me in a state of total concentration	T/F
31. Gave me great insight	T/F	32. Led me to realize that there is meaningfulness to the universe	T/F
33. Caused me to feel that people are sacred	T/F	34. Caused me to view the world as totally desirable	T/F
35. Led me to accept everything	T/F	36. Made the conflicts of life seem to disappear	T/F
37. Caused me to become disorientated in space	T/F	38. Helped me to a greater appreciation of perfection	T/F
39. Helped me to realize that I could never commit suicide	T/F	40. Led me to believe that I could die with dignity	T/F

Now bearing in mind again that there are no right or wrong answers, the scoring of this test is done against a set of answers provided. Match your answers to the table on the next page and score yourself one point for each matching answer.

(circle each correct answer)

1	2	3	4	5	6	7	8	9	10
T	F	T	F	T	F	T	F	T	F
11	12	13	14	15	16	17	18	19	20
T	F	T	F	T	F	T	F	T	F
21	22	23	24	25	26	27	28	29	30
T	F	T	F	T	F	T	F	T	F
31	32	33	34	35	36	37	38	39	40
T	F	T	F	T	F	T	F	T	F

Your Score _____

This is one of the few tests included in this book that is gender impacted, but of course most men and women do tend to view pleasure, happiness and unhappiness in different ways so it is logical that a peak experience test result would vary depending on your gender.

For Women 27 or less: Men 26 or less

If you scored **27 or less** in this test, you are not the type of person to enjoy any form of peak experience. It sounds like you are a very grounded person, which in itself is not a bad thing, but you are denying yourself some real joy if you don't take the time to enjoy some happy experiences to the fullest.

Women 28 – 32: Men 27 - 31

If you scored **between 28 and 32,** you have had the occasional peak experience and you seem to have a balanced life that sits between following rules and following your heart. This is a really healthy way to be, and you should find a successful life just around the corner, if you haven't stumbled on it already.

Women 33 or more: Men 32 or more

If you *scored* **32 or more,** you are a really creative person who has found a fine balance between being tolerant and caring and also assertive where necessary. Your peak experiences come from your ability to live in the moment when appropriate and you also have the skills to succeed in life.

Do You Sabotage Your Success?

This is a multiple-choice test – pick one response to each question.

(Remember no one is grading you – this is for yourself)

1. If you were in debt, it would likely be because
   A) You have a lavish lifestyle
   B) You pay for other people's fun and entertainment
   C) You like to enjoy yourself
   D) You are just not very good at managing money

2. You are not likely to get a promotion at work because
   A) The timing is just not right for you
   B) You are already overworked
   C) You are not interested in extra responsibility
   D) Promotions are for high flyers

3. You are most likely to fight with your partner because
   A) They don't see things your way
   B) They treat you like a doormat
   C) You don't have fun anymore
   D) You often say the wrong thing

4. Your motto would be
   A) Higher, faster and stronger
   B) Give an inch, they take a mile
   C) Live for today
   D) If it ain't broke, don't fix it

5. You are more likely to miss a proposal deadline because
   A) There isn't enough time to do the job properly
   B) You were struggling and no one offered to help you
   C) You got caught up doing other things more interesting
   D) You don't feel the work you have done is worthwhile

6. Hosting a dinner party, you are more likely to overcook the meal because

    A) Guests don't arrive on time
    B) No one offers to help
    C) You are too busy enjoying yourself to notice the time
    D) Your dinner parties are usually a disaster anyway

7. You would rather be

    A) Perfect
    B) Strong
    C) Free
    D) Acceptable

8. You are more likely to drink too much at the office party because you

    A) Can normally hold your drink
    B) Can't say no when someone tops up your glass
    C) Like to have a good time
    D) Have always been a lightweight

9. You are more likely to have a bad time while on holiday because

    A) The resort didn't live up to expectations
    B) It's hard to have fun when you are left to organize everything
    C) It isn't in the stars
    D) You can't let yourself relax and let go

10. You are more likely to be remembered for

    A) Doing it all
    B) Being generous to a fault
    C) Living large
    D) Your modesty

To tally up your score for this test, work out how many "A", "B", "C" or "D" answers you have and which letter you scored the most in.

If you have mostly "A" answers, you are known as a "perfectionist" who is really quite worried about being found out as a bit of a fraud. Your thinking is the "all or nothing" party line and this is not getting you anywhere. Your good enough probably is good enough if you just let it be.

If you have mostly "B" answers, you are like a "pendulum". You have a lot of problems because you are unsure of yourself and don't know how to set boundaries that other people will respect. You will find your mood alternates from being angry to feeling resentful, and you probably feel a bit like the doormat. Your problems can be helped by writing a personal charter and in a journal (later in the book).

If you have mostly "C" answers, you reflect the "connoisseur" of worrying. You are so worried that you might not succeed that you decide to avoid any form of responsibility completely. You would benefit from deciding which goals are important to you and construct a plan to make it happen.

The "D" responders are fairly self-evident. This is a person who has very low self-esteem and always thinks that anything around them that might be wrong is probably their fault. You need to focus on your strengths and to appreciate the achievements you have everyday. Believe it or not, getting out of bed in the morning is an achievement not all of us can master, so write that on your list and add anything else to the list that will make you feel better about yourself.

That's it for the testing in this chapter. You may be feeling a bit bewildered or even overwhelmed at this point, because the mere act of answering questions about yourself sends you on a journey of self-discovery. At this stage, just fill in the table on the opposite page with your final answers for all of this work, as we will refer back to it later on.

If you are feeling a bit uncomfortable, remember that in a situation where you can make changes in your life, or choose not to, that it is your choice and your actions that actually propel your life along the path that you have chosen.

Some of you may feel even worse when you consider that maybe your actions or thoughts in the past might be responsible for current misfortunes, but this is not a blame game, this is the game of cause and effect. For now go and make yourself a cup of hot tea or coffee; sit down somewhere quiet, warm and comfortable, and just let your mind roam freely.

Remind yourself that you are the skipper of your life, that you have every reason to love and accept yourself, because you are a unique and wonderful human being.

An Example of a Gratitude List

I am grateful for...	The reason I am grateful is...
I woke up this morning	I never take my life for granted
I got out of bed this morning	I never take my physical health for granted
I feel good this morning	There have been many mornings when I didn't feel so good
I have a healthy husband I have healthy and happy children	I don't take my family life for granted, or my families health. In the horror stories we hear everyday on the news, I am pleased that everyone in my life is doing well today
I have the benefit of education so I can work from home I have the tools I need to work from home	So many people are locked into work conditions that drain them of their life's energy. I value the fact that I can work from home and I have control over what I do in my day.
I can go outside and enjoy the sun, the fresh air and the country lifestyle in absolute safety We have food in the cupboard	Like the reasons given above I never lose site of the fact that I am really lucky because I live in a place where my health is not compromised by technology, but rather enhanced by it, and we have the staples of life
I have goals to pursue and the means to pursue them	Everyone needs something to work towards in their life – I am hoping to spend time on creative pursuits in the near future

I am grateful for...	The reason I am grateful is...
I am supported emotionally and spiritually by my family	Although I enjoy my own company I love the support network that has evolved around me over the years.
I am so aware of every day as a special gift.	I have faced death many times, and while I don't fear death, I still appreciate every day I am alive.

How Do You Spend Your Day? Or Your Life?

Life Component	Percentage of Time Spent
1. Professional/Work	_____ %
2. Family	_____ %
3. Relationships	_____ %
4. Hobbies/relaxation	_____ %
5. Faith/Spirituality	_____ %
Total Percentage of Time Spent	100 %

There are Others, Then There is Me Exercise

(An example of this exercise)

Label the first column: **Things I do for Others**

Label the second column: **Things I want to do for Me**

Things I do for Others	Things I want to do for Me
1. Drive the carpool on Tuesday/Thursday	1. Take a vacation
2. Pick up David's dry-cleaning	2. Sleep late on weekends
3. Have Mom for supper every Sunday	3. Have a girls' night out
etc	etc

Be exhaustive and list as many things as you can think of. You undoubtedly do a lot of things for others; try to name them all. Conversely, you probably have a lot of things you'd like to do for yourself, get down as many as you can think of.

Reflecting on your list, which side is longer? The "Do for Others" list?

Are there things on the "Do for Me" list that you can start doing now? What about in a week? Will setting clearer boundaries help reduce one side of the list? What about eliminating negativity? Will that take anything off the To Do list? What can you do to have more balance between your lists?

---

www.stephenmark.com

Journaling Page

I appreciate life today because...

I appreciate my job today because...

I appreciate my family today because...

I appreciate my health today because...

I appreciate my abundance today because...

I appreciate _____because
_____
_____
_____
_____and it enables me to _____
_____
_____
_____. This causes me great _____
_____
_____ and gives me the opportunity to _____.

Journaling Page

I appreciate life today because…

I appreciate my job today because…

I appreciate my family today because…

I appreciate my health today because…

I appreciate my abundance today because…

I appreciate _____because
_____
_____
_____
_____and it enables me to _____
_____
_____
_____. This causes me great _____
_____
_____ and gives me the opportunity to _____.

          www.stephenmark.com

Journaling Page

I appreciate life today because…

I appreciate my job today because…

I appreciate my family today because…

I appreciate my health today because…

I appreciate my abundance today because…

I appreciate _____because
_____
_____
____and it enables me to _____
_____
_____. This causes me great _____
_____
_____ and gives me the opportunity to _____.

Blank Journaling Page

Sources Consulted

Accessed City University London News Release, article on "Crisis on the Catwalk: Fashion Models Report Feeling Less Happy and Fulfilled Than Others
http://www.city.ac.uk/news/archive/2007/02_february/12022007_1.html
[January 31st, 2008]

Accessed "Parents or Pop Culture" Childrens' Heroes and Role Models,
http://www-personal.umich.edu/~tmarra/class/anderson.pdf
[February 11, 2008]

Academy of Achievement web site, "Oprah Winfrey Interview" at
http://www.achievement.org/autodoc/page/win0int-1
[January 2, 2008]

Accessed "Models 'lonely with low self-esteem'"
http://www.icWales.co.uk. February 12, 2007.
[January 5, 2008]

Accessed "The Consortium for Research on Emotional Intelligence",
http://www.eiconsortium.org/ [January 7, 2008]

Accessed from the University of Rochester website, white paper on Happiness and despair on the catwalk: Need satisfaction, well-being, and personality adjustment among fashion models
http://www.psych.rochester.edu/
[January 5, 2008]

Accessed "Price of Happiness", http://www.lottery.co.uk/articles/Price-of-happiness.asp
[January 8, 2008]

Accessed "Lottery Winners",
http://www.rotten.com/library/culture/lottery-winners/
[January 20, 2008]

Accessed "Prize Can't Guarantee Happiness",
http://toledoblade.com/apps/pbcs.dll/article?AID=/20060409/NEWS
08/604090315/0/NEWS34
[January 22, 2008]

Accessed J.K. Rowling in *Wikipedia, The Free Encyclopedia.*
http://en.wikipedia.org/w/index.php?title=J._K._Rowling&oldid=2038
03174
[March 31, 2008]

Accessed http://www.jkrowling.com [January 23, 2008]

Accessed "A Fate Worse Than Debt",
http://www.listener.co.nz/issue/3461/columnists/6946/a_fate_worse_t
han_debt.html [January 5, 2008]

Accessed about Oprah - in *Wikipedia, The Free Encyclopedia.*
http://en.wikipedia.org/wiki/Oprah
[January 15, 2008]

Accessed http://www.oprah.com
[January 9, 2008]

Accessed Neuro-linguistic Programming - in *Wikipedia, The Free
Encyclopedia.*
http://en.wikipedia.org/wiki/Neuro-linguistic_programming
[January 15, 2008]

Accessed Consortium for Research on Emotional Intelligence in
Organizations http://www.eiconsortium.org/
[January 5, 2008]

Accessed Cognitive Behavioral Therapy (CBT) in *Wikipedia, The Free
Encyclopedia.*
http://en.wikipedia.org/w/index.php?title=Cognitive_behavioral_therap
y&oldid=202336857
[March 31, 2008]

http://en.wikipedia.org/wiki/Cognitive_behavioral_therapy
[January 15, 2008]

Accessed about Tony http://www.tonyrobbins.com/Home/Home.aspx
[January 12, 2008]

Accessed Law of Attraction - in *Wikipedia, The Free Encyclopedia.*
http://en.wikipedia.org/wiki/Law_of_Attraction
[February 29, 2008]

Accessed Oprah Winfrey - in *Wikipedia, The Free Encyclopedia.*
http://en.wikipedia.org/w/index.php?title=Oprah_Winfrey&oldid=203
321042
[April 6, 2008]

21 Days

To

Creating Your Dream Life

A guide to opening doors and thoughts you never thought possible before…

Stephen J. Mark

Dream Board Publications LLC

Atlanta, Georgia

ACCEPT YOURSELF ~ RESPECT YOURSELF ~ LIVE LIFE EXTRAORDINARILY

Published by

Dream Board Publications LLC, 1353 Riverstone Parkway, Suite 120-252, Canton, GA 30114

Copyright © Stephen J. Mark, 2008

Printed in the United States of America

Library of Congress Control Number: 2008903241

ISBN-13: 978-0-9816275-0-2

ISBN-10:   0-9816275-0-1

DISCLAIMER: The author, publisher and copyright holder expressly disclaim any responsibility for any liability, loss, injury, or risk, personal or otherwise, which is incurred as a consequence, directly or indirectly, of the use and application of any contents of this book and accepts no liabilities for any misuse, misappropriation or abuse of the tools and exercises in this book. There are no expressed or implied warranties attached to this work. The information contained in this book is intended to be for entertainment purposes only and is not for diagnosis, prescription, or treatment of any health disorder whatsoever. This information should not replace consultation with a licensed and competent healthcare professional. If the reader requires personal assistance or advice in any shape or form, a competent and licensed professional should be consulted. Any and all claims are limited to a refund of the price paid for the book minus S&H. By purchasing this book, you agree to the above.

*Each individual's success and outcome depends on his or her background, desire, dedication, implementation and motivation. If you wish to apply the ideas contained in this book, you are taking full responsibility for your actions.

Visit us on the web to order more books or for distribution contacts!

www.stephenmark.com

www.dreamboardpublications.com

BOOKS ARE AVAILABLE AT QUANTITY DISCOUNTS WHEN USED TO PROMOTE PRODUCTS OR SERVICES . FOR INFORMATION PLEASE WRITE TO MARKETING DEPARTMENT, DREAM BOARD PUBLICATIONS LLC, 1353 RIVERSTONE PARKWAY, SUITE 120-252, CANTON, GEORGIA 30114

Contents

       www.stephenmark.com

4

Acknowledgements

There are a number of people I would to thank for their input into this book. First, I would like to thank my wife for her belief and support during this project from its point of conception to final delivery. Next, I would like to thank my mom and dad, friends, and neighbors for their love and support while working on this project.

Thank you and I Love You!

I'd like to thank Tony Robbins and Joseph McClendon III for all their inspiration. Tony, thank you for referencing usable life tools at your seminars. You have always been an inspiration. Both of your inspiring stories have made me change the way I think, feel, and go about life everyday!

A Special Thank You to the Both of you!

I would also like to thank all of the people who have shared their stories in this book, though all names have been changed to protect identities. Any resemblances are coincidental. Without your stories and your own desire for a change in your life, this book would be full of empty, boring pages.

On the technical side, I want to thank Ann Clayton for her graphic design expertise in designing the cover. And to my best friend, Mike Clayton, I want to thank him for his support and consistent brotherhood throughout the years. Lisa Oliver, for all her help and expertise in bringing the material and information together in a recognizable format. I couldn't have done it without you!

Last, but definitely not least, I want to thank you, my readers, because *it is your desire to live the life you want to live* that makes my life all the more worthwhile.

Thank You!

  www.stephenmark.com

Foreword

It is sometimes easy to forget in the world of self-help and self-improvement that every person who looks for something different in their lives all want different things. So their desires are similar, but their measure of success and of achievement are all different. A wealthy banker might want more time with his or her family; a woman who has spent twenty years raising her children might want to go back to school or work; the student might want to travel before beginning a career; and the retiree might want to give something back to his or her community.

This book provides a model for change. It is a system that is flexible enough for you to adapt to, no matter what you want to accomplish in your life. It is also flexible enough to be useful regardless of your current circumstances. Many current self-help books will only help you achieve success in one area of your life, and they tend to include the holistic approach. I hope you will find this book far more suited to your needs than others you might have tried.

I wish you well on your journey to Creating Your Dream Life.

Preface

Are you one of those people who believe that good fortune, success, blooming health and all the perks of a wealthy lifestyle comes to a select few, who somehow have managed to win life's lottery? Are you one of life's ordinary people – humdrum job, humdrum life? Do you believe the gap between where you are and where you want to be is just too big and can never be reached?

<u>**Answer yes to any of the above and you need to read this book.**</u>

You see, too many of us think that success will always be just out of our grasp; that we will never have the good fortune to have a life that fits on the cover of Time magazine, or any publication that we enjoy. What we fail to realize is that **this type of thinking is one of the barriers that is holding us back from our success**. That's right – if you think that you can't succeed and live the life you want to live, you will be right – every time.

You see, the Universe is a wondrous place and whether you believe in it in a spiritual sense or not, the Universe has this way of looking out for you and giving you what you want, all the time. Unfortunately, too many of us spend our time complaining about what we haven't got, and don't take the time to consider that it is our complaints that are coming true in our lives - not our dreams, our desires or our goals. But I am getting ahead of myself. Suffice to say at this point – you have a lot more power to change your life, than you can ever imagine.

Have you ever heard about NLP? NLP stands for Neurolinguistic Programming, which is a personal development system devised in the 1970s. The main idea behind NLP is that it is an individual's thoughts, feelings, actions and experiences that create individual perceptions. It is this perception that impacts the way we act in our daily lives, and it is this perception that can be changed, enabling us to change our lives. WOW, if that were true, and it is, the possibilities for what you could have in your life, are endless.

You have a desire to change your life – otherwise you would not be reading this book. But I am willing to bet that you don't know how to go about it. I am also willing to bet that there is a part of you that is just a bit scared of succeeding – I mean, what would that do to your self-esteem; to your relationships with family, friends and co-workers and to the way you live your life? Change is always a scary prospect, but if you are in control of the change process, then it doesn't have to be a negative experience. This book will show you how you can control your life to the point where you are living where you want to be, and doing what you want to do, rather than what you are doing right now.

I have just one more piece of advice to give you before we begin on your journey to the life you want: Be ready for it. If you are ready, your life could change today – as you are reading this book. And it will change today, because whether you believe in the process this book will teach you, or not, your life will be forever changed because you did read this book. You have nothing to lose and everything to gain from not only reading this book, but also using it as a tool while creating a new blueprint to the life you have only dreamed of. **Let's begin.**

Introduction

Most of us spend our lives looking for "something else" regardless of where we are in our lives at any given time. We could all do with more money, more success, more time, a good relationship, any relationship, a diet that works or an easy way to stop smoking. And no matter where we look, the people we are looking at always seem to have a better life than we do.

This can cause us to feel frustration, envy, bitterness, or resignation. The feelings of frustration are based on the perception that we are not as successful as "they" are; we feel envy at the apparent easy life everyone else seems to have; we feel bitter because we believe that these other people must be so "lucky" and this feeling is often accompanied by the complaint, "how come we don't get the same breaks". Perhaps the saddest emotion this type of observation causes is that of resignation; that feeling of never being good enough, and never being capable of achieving the same happy life that everyone else has or at least that's how it is perceived within ourselves while watching other people around us.

Nothing impacts us more in life than our perceptions of life and people around us, and how we feel about ourselves. We will talk more about perceptions in the first chapter of this book, but for now, you need to appreciate how perceptions filter everything around us. Kind of like a pair of polarized sunglasses, they only allow certain wavelengths of light to come through. They filter out the rest. For example, how would you feel if you had just found out that your neighbor won $100,000 in a lottery draw? Consider the table and responses on the next page:

Feeling	Response
Bitterness	"Just typical isn't it; like they need the money. They're just lucky. I suppose they will just brag around and lord over us even more now, there will be no shutting them up about this one"
Envy	"Wow, I wish I could win that amount of money. Man, I could buy all sorts of things with it – a new boat, a new car, heavens - a new life if I wanted"
Frustration	"Gosh, I am so angry, why can't I get a break like that? I have bills to pay and car repairs I can't pay for. It's not as though they needed the money anyway, why couldn't it have been me?"
Resignation	"Well of course it would happen to them– they are Mister and Misses Successful aren't they? I could never win a lottery; I can't even afford to buy a ticket. I don't know why I am surprised because they obviously deserve it more than me anyway."

Can you relate to any of the statements made by our disgruntled neighbors? Or do you have a more positive outlook on life?

Let's consider some positive responses to the same situation. See which table better describes you.

Feeling	Response
Happiness	"Wow, that is so great – they really deserve this win. I must go over and congratulate them, maybe now they will be able to afford a holiday or something special for themselves"
Surprise	"Wow, I never knew anyone that won a large sum of money like that in a lottery before. Maybe I should start buying tickets"
Genuine goodwill	"That is just wonderful. If anybody deserved to win a nice sum of money it is our neighbors. They are such nice people and I hope they can do something positive for themselves with it"
Thankfulness	"I am so pleased that the win went to such a nice family. They have had so many trials and tribulations lately, this will seem like a gift from the heavens. I am so thankful it went to a family that really needed it"

As you can see, these tables show eight completely different responses to the same situation and this is not an exhaustive list. The tables don't mention anger, hatred, anxiety, greed, or a multitude of other feelings that could be generated by the one event.

A second aspect that we can learn from this example is that our feelings regulate our responses and behavior. If I asked you to name a feeling that applied to any one of the eight responses illustrated, I am sure you would not have too much trouble working out which one was

                    www.stephenmark.com

which. What if we added a behavior column to the same example? We would get something that looked like this:

Feeling	Behavior
Bitterness	Goes off to get another beer from the fridge and when he sees his neighbor later in the day he just ignores him.
Envy	Goes around to visit the neighbors to find out what they will be buying and how they will spend it, and see if there is any chance he can get some money directed his way.
Frustration	Slams around the house for a while, and then goes off to meet with some friends. Turns back up at home a lot later and smelling like booze.
Resignation	Sits quietly in his room, wondering if his life will ever get any better. But he doesn't think it will, so he is probably right.
Happiness	Whips up a batch of cookies and goes over to visit the neighbors, happy to share their good fortune and to offer congratulations.
Surprise	Starts looking at the statistics about the chance of winning the lottery and decides it probably wouldn't hurt to get a ticket even though the odds of winning are quite low, because "you have to be in it to win it".
Thankfulness	Pops round to visit the neighbors, just to say how pleased he is for them. Later he prays and gives thanks for the neighbors' good fortune.